**New Directions for
Higher Education**

Martin Kramer
EDITOR-IN-CHIEF

Managing for Innovation

Theodore S. Glickman
Susan C. White
EDITORS

Number 137 • Spring 2007
Jossey-Bass
San Francisco

MANAGING FOR INNOVATION
Theodore S. Glickman, Susan C. White (eds.)
New Directions for Higher Education, no. 137
Martin Kramer, Editor-in-Chief

Microfilm copies of issues and articles are available in 16mm and 35mm, as well as microfiche in 105mm, through University Microfilms Inc., 300 North Zeeb Road, Ann Arbor, Michigan 48106-1346.

NEW DIRECTIONS FOR HIGHER EDUCATION (ISSN 0271-0560, electronic ISSN 1536-0741) is part of The Jossey-Bass Higher and Adult Education Series and is published quarterly by Wiley Subscription Services, Inc., A Wiley Company, at Jossey-Bass, 989 Market Street, San Francisco, California 94103-1741. Periodicals Postage Paid at San Francisco, California, and at additional mailing offices. POSTMASTER: Send address changes to New Directions for Higher Education, Jossey-Bass, 989 Market Street, San Francisco, California 94103-1741.

New Directions for Higher Education is indexed in Current Index to Journals in Education (ERIC); Higher Education Abstracts.

SUBSCRIPTIONS cost $80 for individuals and $195 for institutions, agencies, and libraries. See ordering information page at end of journal.

EDITORIAL CORRESPONDENCE should be sent to the Editor-in-Chief, Martin Kramer, 2807 Shasta Road, Berkeley, California 94708-2011.

Cover photograph © Digital Vision

www.josseybass.com

CONTENTS

EDITORS' NOTES   1
Theodore S. Glickman, Susan C. White

1. Application of the Baldrige Model for Innovation in   5
Higher Education
Julie A. Furst-Bowe, Roy A. Bauer
Innovation helped the University of Wisconsin-Stout to be the first
school to receive the Malcolm Baldrige National Quality Award.

2. Innovation in Higher Education: A Case Study of the   15
Western Governors University
Kevin Kinser
Through innovation, Western Governors University overcame the
challenges associated with competency-based distance education.

3. Universal Design Across the Curriculum   27
Robbin Zeff
The author offers a comprehensive review of the innovative application
of universal design in the higher education environment.

4. A Challenging Journey: From Leadership Courses to   45
Leadership Foundation for Higher Education
Robin Middlehurst
The U.K. Leadership Foundation for Higher Education has innovated
by offering comprehensive leadership development across institutions.

5. Higher Education Assessment: Linking Accreditation   59
Standards and the Malcolm Baldrige Criteria
Brent D. Ruben
Linking accreditation standards to the Malcolm Baldrige criteria creates
an innovative continuous improvement environment.

6. Information Technology: A Contributor to Innovation in   85
Higher Education
Ted Dodds
The author provides insights into using information technology to
foster excellence through innovative communities, institutional
practices, and infrastructure.

7. Innovation in Higher Education: Implications for   97
the Future
Susan C. White, Theodore S. Glickman
The authors explain why adaptability, maturity, cost structure, and
efficiency are critical to innovation in higher education.

INDEX   107

EDITORS' NOTES

Not long ago, management thinker Peter Drucker (1997) noted that "the most important area for developing new concepts, methods, and practices will be in the management of society's knowledge resources—specifically, education and health care, both of which are today overadministered and undermanaged" (p. 20). This volume of New Directions for Higher Education reflects on that theme while recognizing that while the concepts, methods, and practices needed may be new, many of the challenges that higher education administrators face today are not: administering tighter budgets, demonstrating outcomes in an environment of increased accountability, and providing equitable opportunities for access to higher education. Solving these problems may require innovative managerial practices, or at least the innovative application of existing practices to new arenas, recognizing that observer Arthur Levine (1980) was right to remind us that "much that we call innovation is in fact renovation, trying the ideas of the past once again" (p. 4). Whether the management ideas and experience discussed in this volume are truly innovative or primarily renovative in nature is less important than the knowledge that they have helped academic administrators better manage their resources as they continue to grapple with the realities of operating in the current environment.

Innovation springs from the fresh examination of processes and practices that may have become stale and stagnated, offering institutions increased flexibility by presenting them with new alternatives for improving the efficiency and effectiveness of their operations. The chapters in this volume examine creative approaches to accomplishing these goals in a variety of academic institutions.

In Chapter One, Julie A. Furst-Bowe and Roy A. Bauer present a process that, when institutionalized, can generate continuous and systematic gains in quality and innovation. They view innovation as vital to improving both operating efficiencies and learning effectiveness. The University of Wisconsin-Stout implemented this process and became the first university to receive the Malcolm Baldrige National Quality Award. This award demonstrates a sustained commitment to processes that result in improved quality and institutionalized means of developing new approaches to address deficiencies.

The creation of Western Governors University (WGU) marked a truly innovative approach to higher education through its application of what were then new technologies and its competency-based model of demonstrating

NEW DIRECTIONS FOR HIGHER EDUCATION, no. 137, Spring 2007 © Wiley Periodicals, Inc.
Published online in Wiley InterScience (www.interscience.wiley.com) • DOI: 10.1002/he.241

learning success. Kevin Kinser tells the story of WGU in Chapter Two. In this case, the founding administration had to deal with some of the negatives of being innovative. For example, it took longer than anticipated to earn accreditation. Despite its early struggles, WGU is an active institution today.

Surprisingly, federal legislation enacted in the 1970s and 1980s that mandated physical access to public facilities for the disabled has resulted in innovations today in higher education. Universal design, originally conceived to address the issues of physical accessibility, is being applied to educational design. Robbin Zeff examines the multifaceted implications of universal design for learning in Chapter Three. The same principles that allowed those with physical limitations to gain easier access to public spaces are now being employed to provide increased accessibility in higher education.

The creation of new programs that span organizational boundaries often calls for innovative approaches in both curricular and operational design. Such was the case when the Leadership Foundation for Higher Education was established in the United Kingdom. Robin Middlehurst provides insight into the challenges and solutions in Chapter Four. The foundation supports research and education in its ongoing quest to promote and support excellence in leadership and management and leadership development.

Assessment is a reality in higher education, as institutions face increasing pressures regarding the education of students. In Chapter Five, Brent D. Ruben considers ways in which the Malcolm Baldrige criteria can be tied to accreditation standards. Not only can the process support continuous improvement and innovation; it can also be linked directly to the metrics and reports mandated by accrediting agencies. Thus, the examination of the results provides regular opportunities for innovation in curricular development.

Ted Dodds presents a model of information technology as a direct contributor to innovation in higher education in Chapter Six. It is important to remember that hardware and software alone cannot solve problems and will not foster innovation unless they are applied properly. It is the effective and efficient deployment of information technology tools that can help support innovation.

Finally, in Chapter Seven, we provide a comprehensive overview of the implications of innovation in higher education, concluding that if an institution does not search for new approaches or seek ways to use current solutions in new ways or settings, it will not survive. In today's environment, innovation is mandatory; it is not for the few but for all.

Innovation, whether in the form of new ideas or the imaginative application of old methods, can provide the means by which universities not merely hang on but thrive. We trust that the chapters collected here will help advance the cause of innovation and trigger a new round of innovation in an upward spiral of novel programs and processes as higher education advances to new heights in this century.

Theodore S. Glickman
Susan C. White
Editors

References

Drucker, P. "The Future Has Already Happened." *Harvard Business Review,* Sept.–Oct. 1997, pp. 20–24.

Levine, A. *Why Innovation Fails: The Institutionalization and Termination of Innovation in Higher Education.* Albany, N.Y.: SUNY Press, 1980.

THEODORE S. GLICKMAN *is associate professor of decision sciences in the George Washington University Business School and senior fellow in the Homeland Security Policy Institute.*

SUSAN C. WHITE *is assistant professor of decision sciences in the Business School at George Washington University and co-deputy director of Writing in the Disciplines.*

1

The Malcolm Baldrige Quality guideposts provide a comprehensive model for systematic quality improvement and innovation in colleges and universities.

Application of the Baldrige Model for Innovation in Higher Education

Julie A. Furst-Bowe, Roy A. Bauer

Technological advances, heightened student expectations, shifting student demographics, stakeholder demands for accountability, and new vehicles for educational delivery are all current challenges driving the need for innovation in higher education (Jurow, 2006). It is extremely difficult to meet these challenges given the environment of limited financial resources, and it is clear that institutions must reexamine traditional methods of operation and innovate in order to remain viable now and in the future (Sorensen, Furst-Bowe, and Moen, 2005). *Innovation* is defined as making meaningful change to improve an organization's processes and services and creating new value for the organization's stakeholders. It should focus on leading the organization to new dimensions of performance (Baldrige National Quality Program, 2006).

No longer strictly the purview of research and development departments, innovation is critical in higher education institutions for providing increasing educational value to students and improving the effectiveness of all learning-centered processes and the efficiency with which support processes assist these learning-centered processes. Colleges and universities should be led and managed in such a way that innovation becomes a natural part of the culture and daily operations as innovation builds on the accumulated knowledge of all faculty and staff members. The ability to rapidly disseminate and capitalize on this knowledge is critical to driving institutional improvement (Baldrige National Quality Program, 2006).

New Directions for Higher Education, no. 137, Spring 2007 © Wiley Periodicals, Inc.
Published online in Wiley InterScience (www.interscience.wiley.com) • DOI: 10.1002/he.242

Driving innovation and implementing sustained improvements are often extremely difficult for colleges and universities. To some degree, each institution in its own way may consider itself to be somewhat innovative. Every college and university can produce an array of press releases describing new programs and activities that are different from the academic norm and break new ground (at least for that institution) and that talented people have designed for good purposes. However, for the most part, these new activities and other changes are random, not systematic. Few institutions have gained much control over the outcomes produced as a result of innovation, and many institutions that invest considerable time and effort in attempts to improve performance often fall back into long-established patterns (Tagg, 2005). It is clear that most institutions lack a systematic framework that allows them to effectively manage change, encourage innovation, and obtain increasingly positive results from their efforts.

There is a process and systematic method by which change and innovative new concepts occur. New concepts appear because of fortunate circumstances: once-disparate technologies combine to create new value, the environment contains essential elements, and people are prepared to recognize new possibilities. This situation, coupled with a cultural or economic crisis or a compelling vision of the future, provides a catalyst for change and innovation (Bauer, Collar, and Tang, 1992). Clearly, higher education contains all the essential elements for change and innovation. What is needed is a tool or model to provide a systematic process to drive and manage change. The Malcolm Baldrige Criteria for Performance Excellence provide an effective model for this purpose.

The Baldrige Criteria for Performance Excellence

Managing for innovation is one of the core values of the Malcolm Baldrige criteria. The criteria provide a comprehensive structure for educational institutions to align their mission, vision, values, goals, and strategic challenges with the resources essential for long-term improvement. First developed to increase the competitiveness of U.S. manufacturing companies in the late 1980s, the criteria have evolved and have become the de facto definition of performance excellence worldwide (Hoisington and Vaneswaran, 2005).

The criteria were extensively reviewed and modified for educational and health care organizations in the mid-1990s. The core values and concepts of the education criteria are embodied in seven categories: Leadership; Strategic Planning; Student, Stakeholder, and Market Focus; Measurement, Analysis, and Knowledge Management; Faculty and Staff Focus; Process Management; and Organizational Performance Results. Education institutions may use the criteria for internal improvement or address them in a written application and submit the application for review, scoring, and national award consideration. Schools, colleges, and universities could apply for the Malcolm Baldrige National Quality Award beginning in 1999. Over

NEW DIRECTIONS FOR HIGHER EDUCATION • DOI: 10.1002/he

the past seven years, numerous postsecondary institutions have used the Baldrige values and criteria as a management framework to drive innovation and change in key criteria areas. When an institution can clarify the roles of leadership and planning and clearly articulate the outcomes it seeks, it is more likely to succeed in embedding innovation into the culture (Jurow, 2006).

Baldrige Influence on Academic Accreditation

The Baldrige framework has begun to have a significant influence on the approaches that regional accrediting associations use (Ruben, 2004). For example, the concept of quality improvement is at the heart of the Southern Association of Colleges and Schools Commission on Colleges' philosophy of accreditation. Each institution applying for accreditation or renewal of accreditation is required to develop a quality enhancement plan. Engaging the wider academic community and addressing one or more key institutional issues, the plan must be focused and succinct. It describes a carefully designed and focused course of action that addresses a well-defined topic or key issue and brings about needed changes related to enhancing student learning and performance.

The Higher Learning Commission of the North Central Association of Colleges and Schools has developed and implemented an alternative accreditation process supporting institutions using continuous improvement systems (Spangehl, 2004). This process, named the Academic Quality Improvement Program (AQIP), shifts the focus of accreditation from inputs, such as SAT scores, faculty credentials, or number of library volumes, to performance, or how well an institution meets the long-term needs of its students and stakeholders (Spangehl, 2004). Currently more than one hundred postsecondary institutions have selected this method of accreditation, and the number continues to increase each year as institutions recognize the value of this framework to assist them in making the changes needed to remain viable in the current higher education environment.

To restructure accreditation, AQIP did not simply substitute a set of output indexes for the traditional input requirements. Instead, it followed the Baldrige approach of delineating core values and criteria and asking institutions to identify their own performance measures within each of these criteria areas (Spangehl, 2004). Like Baldrige, AQIP is a nonprescriptive approach, keeping the institution focused on managing change and improving performance. It enables institutions that have embraced continuous quality improvement to incorporate accreditation into their everyday operations and activities so accreditation does not become a single event but a systematic and ongoing process.

In addition to the regional accrediting organizations, many program-specific accrediting bodies such as the Accreditation Board for Engineering and Technology and the National Council for Accreditation of Teacher

Education are moving in the direction of an outcomes-based, continuous review process rather than the traditional periodic assessment to ensure a university's or college's ability to achieve its mission. Over the past decade, the Baldrige criteria have influenced accreditation standards and criteria in a number of disciplines.

Currently, three postsecondary institutions have successfully implemented the Baldrige criteria, submitted formal applications to the Baldrige program, and received the Malcolm Baldrige National Quality Award: the University of Wisconsin-Stout (also an AQIP institution), the Monfort College of Business at the University of Northern Colorado, and Richland College, a large community college in Dallas, Texas. Although each of these institutions has a distinct mission and serves a very different student population, each was able to use the criteria and process to introduce new approaches to improve student learning and organizational performance. These approaches were sustained, and over time they produced high-level results in areas such as student learning and performance, stakeholder satisfaction, faculty and staff well-being, and overall organizational effectiveness.

Innovation at the University of Wisconsin-Stout

The University of Wisconsin-Stout (UW-Stout), a comprehensive university with eight thousand students located in northwestern Wisconsin, was one of the first universities to adopt the Baldrige criteria and in 2001 became the first postsecondary institution to receive the Baldrige award. Part of the University of Wisconsin System, UW-Stout is a special-mission institution focused on career-oriented academic programs. With more than a decade of experience in systematic quality improvement, it has been able to drive innovation in several areas of the campus, including academic, administrative, and student support services, and create new systems for shared leadership, strategic planning, student performance, and determining stakeholder satisfaction.

The typical leadership structure in higher education is bureaucratic in nature and more prone to conflict than innovation or collaboration (Srikanthan and Dalrymple, 2002). Few college or university leaders have clearly defined their institution's goals and ways to achieve them (Massey, 2003). However, one of the Baldrige core values is visionary leadership, in which senior leaders set directions and create a student-focused, learning-oriented campus climate. The Baldrige criteria ask how senior leaders communicate with faculty and staff through open two-way communication and how senior leaders create a focus on action to accomplish the organization's objectives. UW-Stout developed an innovative approach to leadership that addresses the Baldrige model. The university leadership system removes organizational complications and inhibitors, encourages responsive multidirectional communication, and flattens the organizational structure through broad involvement of all governance bodies and stakeholder groups.

NEW DIRECTIONS FOR HIGHER EDUCATION • DOI: 10.1002/he

The Chancellor's Advisory Council is the core of the leadership system. The group meets biweekly and has twenty members, including administrators, faculty, staff, and student governance leaders. These members of the senior leadership team provide the communication conduit to and from their respective organizations, resulting in strong communication linkages, participatory decision making, and enhanced opportunity for meaningful roles in shared governance issues (Sorensen, Furst-Bowe, and Moen, 2005). No major decision or allocation of resources is made on campus without first being discussed by the council. For example, when UW-Stout decided to become a laptop campus (beginning with the Fall 2002 semester, each incoming freshman was required to have a laptop computer), this initiative was discussed extensively by the council, with the faculty voicing concerns regarding mediated classrooms and training opportunities and the students voicing concerns related to hardware, software, and program costs. As a result, the campus was able to address all concerns prior to implementation of this major change initiative. Other Baldrige-winning institutions have also established collaborative leadership systems that include significant roles for faculty, students and other stakeholders.

Effective planning is essential in making fundamental changes in an institution (Jurow, 2006). However, in most postsecondary institutions, planning is limited to enrollment management and academic program development. Many important areas, such as educational and support process management, receive little attention (Massey, 2003). In the area of strategic planning, the Baldrige criteria call for a systematic strategy development process that includes a SWOT (strengths, weaknesses, opportunities, and threats) analysis of the institution and addresses key factors including changes in student and community demographics, technology, and markets, as well as peer and competitor institutions. Strategy development might use various types of forecasts, projections, scenarios, or other approaches to envisioning the future for purposes of identifying strategic objectives, making decisions, and allocating resources. The process for converting strategic objectives into action plans, establishing goals relative to leadership benchmarks, and measuring the success of action plans through key performance indicators are also important aspects of the criteria (Baldrige National Quality Program, 2006). Over the past decade, UW-Stout has implemented a robust strategic planning process responding to multiple aspects of the Baldrige criteria. The process is framed by the development of mission, vision, and values statements and incorporates situational analysis, including stakeholder visioning. Strategic objectives require the deployment of action plans and six-month reviews to monitor and alter implementation to ensure success. The unique strengths of the process are its demonstrated ability to integrate long-term plans, short-term plans, and resource allocation. It is also characterized by broad participation by both internal and external stakeholders (Sorensen, Furst-Bowe, and Moen, 2005).

Three primary groups provide support to the UW-Stout strategic planning system. The Chancellor's Advisory Council is the key leadership group, aligning planning with resource allocation and deploying agreed-on action plans. The Strategic Planning Group, which consists of the Chancellor's Advisory Council plus additional faculty, staff, and student representatives, is responsible for maintaining viable mission, vision, and values statements and long-term goals. The group also develops strategic objectives under each goal area, known as key performance indicators, and monitors the implementation of action plans. The Office of Budget, Planning and Analysis includes the functions of institutional research, fiscal analysis, annual operating budget, and capital budget development. This combination of functions has strengthened the use of data in planning and decision making, aligned resources with strategic objectives and their accompanying action plans, and supported the process to measure university performance against key performance indicators.

Action plans are used to ensure that the appropriate steps are taken to complete each strategic objective. Each action plan includes the proposed initiative; its linkage to the strategic plan; the high-level actions that need to be completed; the positions, individuals, or groups that will be responsible for each step; the time line; the resources required; and the key performance indicators associated with the strategic objective. All action plans are monitored every six months by the Strategic Planning Group. Since UW-Stout began developing action plans in the late 1990s, more than fifty strategic objectives have been achieved in areas related to technology integration, campus climate, gender equity, globalization, and graduate education. A recent strategic objective related to academic program development resulted in the establishment of the Curriculum Innovation Center, where faculty members from various disciplines receive release time or summer session salary to collaborate on new program and course development in areas such as nanotechnology, neuroscience, and interactive digital environments— program improvements supporting UW-Stout's focused mission.

In the area of student learning and performance, the Baldrige criteria require that institutions provide current levels and trends in key areas or indicators of student learning and improvements in student learning. To address these criteria, UW-Stout measures student learning and progress beginning when students enroll at the institution and continuing well after graduation. Incoming freshmen complete placement tests in key subject areas, such as math, English, and a foreign language.

Each academic program has developed a set of established objectives and identified appropriate methods to assess student achievement of those objectives, including course-embedded assessments, standardized exams, electronic portfolios, and evaluations from experiential learning supervisors. General education abilities are measured by the ACT CAAP (Collegiate Assessment of Academic Proficiency) exam, which is administered annually to a large sample of upperclassmen. Instructors of general education also administer

NEW DIRECTIONS FOR HIGHER EDUCATION • DOI: 10.1002/he

course-embedded assessments, and seniors complete an assessment of their general education skills. Results of assessments are reviewed by instructors and program directors on an annual basis, and written plans for improving teaching and learning are developed and shared with faculty members and administrators.

Most colleges and universities have few data about how well they are serving current and future stakeholders (Massey, 2003). Collecting these data and analyzing trends to determine changing needs of key stakeholders, including alumni and employers, provide UW-Stout with valuable information for refining and improving programs and services. Many times, these data surface needed changes and areas where innovation is required to better serve these key constituent groups. Alumni are surveyed one and five years following graduation using the ACT Alumni Outcomes Survey and program-specific evaluations developed by the institution. Employer feedback on graduate skills is also considered critical as UW-Stout's mission emphasizes career preparation. For the past decade, more than 95 percent of graduates have been placed in career positions, and the university has more employers recruiting students on campus and participating in career fairs, advisory committees, and other related activities than other universities in its peer group. Employers are also formally surveyed to determine their satisfaction level with graduate knowledge, skills, and abilities and identify innovative areas of curricular revision, new program development, or improved services, including expansion of video and virtual interviewing services.

The development and implementation of appropriate measurement systems and performance indicators was essential to UW-Stout's successful application of the Baldrige criteria. The quantity of measures evaluated is not important; the key is measuring performance of entire systems end to end. Historically UW-Stout had a reputation for being a data-driven, fact-based institution. But until the institution began systematic application of the Baldrige criteria, senior leaders did not understand how all the data and measures should be viewed, organized, and reviewed to develop a comprehensive, fact-based assessment of the effectiveness of the organization's key processes, mission, and goals.

Prior to adopting the Baldrige criteria, UW-Stout had too many metrics in some areas and inadequate metrics in other areas, and the institution could not identify what the core set of metrics was that defined overall system performance. Furthermore, while UW-Stout had comparative data related to the other University of Wisconsin System campuses, there were few comparative data to assess performance or set goals relative to key competitors or leaders in the field. Therefore, no one knew if the goals set by the institution would enable the university to establish clear leadership in important strategic areas. With Baldrige as the model, the university was able to align the entire data and measurement system to support the overall mission and programs of the university more adequately and, using trends and comparative data, ascertain and drive continuous and systematic performance improvement.

Keys to Successful Change Management

Historically, colleges and universities that have made innovative changes in the areas suggested here have done so when the very existence of the institution was threatened by forces that disrupted the existing equilibrium (Tagg, 2005). UW-Stout, for example, began transforming its systems and processes following a no-confidence vote against the current chancellor more than a decade ago. The greatest challenge for advocates of innovation in higher education has been to break through the defenses of institutions that are well established and not threatened with imminent destruction. An institution that is structured in the conventional manner is largely designed to stay the way it is—to maintain the status quo.

This is true with any organization in any sector. Every organization implements structures, business controls, and other disciplines to be able to manage consistently and support its mission and purpose. Organizations that have stood intact the longest or have a history of long-term success become the most ingrained in their culture and methods of carrying out their mission. Structures evolve to the point where their existence depends on maintaining the status quo. This bureaucracy tends to stifle new ideas and concepts, and it takes strong leadership and a systematic approach to change and neutralize the bureaucratic forces standing in the way.

Institutions that have been successful in driving innovation and managing change generally share four common elements: commitment and continued support from top leadership, systematic planning methods, inclusive and participatory processes, and effective, multidirectional communication (Sorensen, 2003). There is one other important element for driving innovation and change: it must be driven by individuals with line authority (presidents, vice presidents, deans, or department chairs) and not delegated to a committee, special task force, quality improvement office, or other staff function. In order to engage faculty and staff in innovative efforts, there must be a sense of priority from people in senior positions. Although many people believe that initiatives are best supported and most likely to be successful when they emerge from and are owned by the faculty and staff, many initiatives fail or are not sustained if there is not a continued sense of their importance by senior administrators (Kezar, 2005).

One way to model innovation is in the way the president works with the cabinet, as well as other senior administrative teams and governance groups. Presidents, provosts, and deans on innovative campuses do not make unilateral decisions but work with other members of their leadership teams, as well as faculty and staff members, to plan, make decisions, and allocate resources. As people on campus witness these shared processes and decisions, they realize that collaboration is part of the fabric of the institution (Kezar, 2005).

NEW DIRECTIONS FOR HIGHER EDUCATION • DOI: 10.1002/he

Application of the Baldrige model, applied with commitment and over time, results in a leadership environment that fosters empowerment, innovation, and a shared vision among faculty, staff, and administration.

Lessons Learned

Even with these four elements in place, the path to innovation is not without risk and is not always smooth as an organization assimilates new processes (Sorensen, Furst-Bowe, and Moen, 2005). Especially in higher education, there is a strong need to discuss, debate, and deliberate on the merits of even the smallest proposed change. Many within the academy question the relevance of the Baldrige model. Faculty members claim that the true worth of a degree cannot be measured, that faculty expertise is the only important factor in determining quality, and that universities exist to create and preserve knowledge rather than to serve stakeholders (Massey, 2003). Even among Baldrige-winning institutions, the criteria and awards process were questioned, the reputation and performance of recipients were analyzed, and the rights of the faculty were emphasized. Not all administrators, faculty, and staff bought in to the process at the same rate or with the same levels of commitment and enthusiasm.

In any successful change process, it is necessary to begin with a few senior leaders and other key individuals who are prepared to recognize possibilities, look for solutions to a problem, or capitalize on an opportunity. These core groups of individuals become the catalysts that initiate the actions for initial completion of small successes. Small successes begin to lend credibility to the actions and generate positive momentum for change and greater buy-in from faculty and staff members. Strong leadership support to stay the course is required to support the change agents and keep negative individuals from disrupting the actions (Bauer, Collar, and Tang, 1992). At UW-Stout, it took approximately three years for faculty and staff to realize the benefits of the new leadership system, planning process, and other innovations.

In addition, many institutions believe that they would have to reinvent themselves and overhaul all of their systems and processes before they could begin to apply the Baldrige framework. However, the criteria are nonprescriptive and can be adapted to all types of higher education institutions. Each institution can determine the extent and depth to initially infuse the Baldrige criteria and can build on the existing inventory of institutional strengths (Sorensen, Furst-Bowe, and Moen, 2005). It takes a number of years to fully implement the criteria, but institutions that take the first steps and focus on one or two of the criteria areas may begin to realize positive results in a matter of months.

It is clear from all indicators that both public and private colleges and universities will continue to face severe fiscal issues, more demands from governing boards and state legislatures on efficiencies and accountability

NEW DIRECTIONS FOR HIGHER EDUCATION • DOI: 10.1002/he

measures, and greater pressure to hold down the rising cost of education. Senior leaders will be forced to find answers or at least explore measures to ensure students and stakeholders that they understand and are addressing the issues (Sorensen, Furst-Bowe, and Moen, 2005). Although no quality improvement model is without its limitations, college and university leaders will find the Baldrige model useful because it provides a tested framework for institutions to begin the process of systematic assessment and improvement through change initiatives. Ideas and approaches that have not been tried and tested, or that have been tried before and failed, have a better chance of implementation success using the Baldrige model because the model helps to align and integrate processes and synthesize the important performance indicators across the organization.

References

Baldrige National Quality Program. *Education Criteria for Performance Excellence.* Gaithersburg, Md.: National Institute for Standards and Technology, 2006.
Bauer, R., Collar, E., and Tang, V. *The Silverlake Project: Transformation at IBM.* New York: Oxford University Press, 1992.
Hoisington, S. H., and Vaneswaran, S. A. *Implementing Strategic Change: Tools for Transforming an Organization.* New York: McGraw-Hill, 2005.
Jurow, S. "Set in Your Ways?" *Business Officer,* 2006, 39(8), 18–22.
Kezar, A. "Moving from I to We." *Change,* 2005, 37(6), 50–57.
Massey, W. F. *Honoring the Trust: Quality and Cost Containment in Higher Education.* Bolton, Mass.: Anker Publishing, 2003.
Ruben, B. D. *Pursuing Excellence in Higher Education: Eight Fundamental Challenges.* San Francisco: Jossey-Bass, 2004.
Sorensen, C. W. "University of Wisconsin–Stout: 2001 Malcolm Baldrige National Quality Award." *Journal of Innovative Management,* 2003, 8(2), 41–78.
Sorensen, C. W., Furst-Bowe, J. A., and Moen, D. (eds). *Quality and Performance Excellence in Higher Education: Baldrige on Campus.* Bolton, Mass.: Anker Publishing, 2005.
Spangehl, S. D. "The North Central Association of Colleges and Schools Academic Quality Improvement Project (AQIP)." In B. D. Ruben (ed.), *Pursuing Excellence in Higher Education: Eight Fundamental Challenges.* San Francisco: Jossey-Bass, 2004.
Srikanthan, G., and Dalrymple, J. F. "Developing a Holistic Model for Quality in Higher Education." *Quality in Higher Education,* 2002, 8(3), 215–224.
Tagg, J. "Venture Colleges." *Change,* 2005, 37(1), 34–43.

JULIE A. FURST-BOWE *is the provost and vice chancellor for academic and student affairs at the University of Wisconsin–Stout in Menomonie, Wisconsin.*

ROY A. BAUER *is the president and chief operating officer at Pemstar, Incorporated in Rochester, Minnesota.*

2

Western Governors University shows how both foreseen and unforeseen challenges shape innovative management responses.

Innovation in Higher Education: A Case Study of the Western Governors University

Kevin Kinser

In 1995, a few western governors saw a future with ever increasing numbers of students coming to college. They looked at the state budget and saw no money forthcoming to build new campuses to handle the crush. And they saw students being denied access to higher education because of the unwillingness of existing institutions to take advantage of technology and distance learning. Since these governors were also sharply critical of traditional higher education and doubted its ability to respond to these challenges, they decided to create their own university that would do just that. They called this new institution Western Governors University (WGU) and claimed that its competency-based, distance education model would serve as a catalyst for change in higher education (Western Governors Association, 1996).

It was an institution of higher education that, while still little more than a four-page vision statement, had colleges and universities concerned about their own survival. Before even a single student was enrolled, its impact was being compared to that of the GI Bill. No courses had been listed in its

Information on the history and early development of Western Governors University (WGU) is based on research I conducted between 1997 and 1999 (Kinser, 1999). In 2004, I revisited WGU and interviewed current staff. These interviews informed the conclusions in this chapter.

catalogue, yet people were calling it the most ambitious distance-learning initiative in the United States. Barely begun, WGU captivated politicians, business executives, academics, accreditors, and technology advocates (Marchese, 1998). They saw the future of higher education, and it was WGU.

It was an unnerving future for them to consider. There would be no faculty, no classes, and no campus. The curriculum would be defined by demonstrated competency, not credit hours. Performance, not grades, would be the coin of the realm. Competition between institutions would be based on price and service, and a host of independent education providers would step forward to meet the demands of the market. In the center would stand WGU, credentialing student learning and establishing standards. The governors predicted their new university would soon be serving tens of thousands of students. A transformation of higher education was at hand.

It did not work out that way.

WGU was slow to get off the ground. It took four years from the original discussions the governors had about forming the new university for it to officially open, and it struggled with enrollment problems throughout its early existence. Few independent providers were interested in mapping their courses to WGU competencies. It took longer than expected to earn accreditation. Revenue did not match predictions. In sharp contrast to early assertions of the competitive advantages posed by the WGU model, critics of the new university began to question its viability as an academic institution (Carnevale, 2000; Kinser, 2002; Meyer, 2005).

External events and bad timing also cut short the WGU juggernaut. The burst of the dot-com bubble put an end to hyperbolic predictions of distance-learning proponents everywhere. Big efforts at capitalizing on technology to create new organizational forms for education—the California Virtual University, HungryMinds, Fathom, and many others—collapsed (Zemsky and Massey, 2004). At the same time, traditional institutions began devoting an increasing amount of energy to their own distance-learning operations (Allen and Seaman, 2004). The draw of WGU as a radical virtual university experiment lessened as the transformative technological rhetoric of the 1990s was replaced by the practical, daily routine of technology in the 2000s. From a position of such prominence, WGU dropped off the radar for most observers of higher education.

The story might end there, serving as yet another example of how difficult it is to change higher education. Today, however, WGU is an active institution. It has largely solved its enrollment problems. Over five thousand students are enrolled in a quite successful teacher education program, in addition to a few other targeted programs in information technology and business. It earned national accreditation from the Distance Education and Training Council in 2001 and regional accreditation from the Northwest Association of Schools and Colleges in 2003. Accreditation, though, did not result in a loss of its nontraditional status. WGU does not employ traditional faculty and does not offer conventional academic courses. External providers are contracted for almost all WGU learning resources. And it has maintained its commitment to assessment of competencies rather than awarding of grades as the measure of learning for its degrees.

WGU still remains a significant player in political circles. Several founding governors have moved into positions of national importance, including President George W. Bush (Texas), U.S. Secretary of Health and Human Services Michael Leavitt (Utah), and Senator Ben Nelson (Nebraska). These connections have been put to apparent good use. WGU participates in the U.S. Department of Education Distance Education Demonstration Program. The president of WGU is a member of a presidential panel on the future of higher education. WGU has received federal grants and earmarks and is mentioned by name in the Higher Education Act. A degree from the WGU Teacher Education program is accepted for local certification purposes in nearly every state in the Union. Although WGU is no longer an icon of higher education transformation, it has nonetheless become the innovative institution its planners envisioned: a radically different model for higher education, firmly established as a legitimate option for postsecondary education in the United States.

The Emerging WGU

The founders and developers of WGU reconceptualized the organization and evaluation of learning in a distance education environment. But the WGU model did not emerge from whole cloth. Although from the beginning the governors had a fairly good idea of what they wanted WGU to be, and much of their original vision remains today, the creation of a university out of the vision saw modification and compromise. In fact, much of the explanation for the slow start of WGU can be attributed to the time it took to extricate the emerging institution from problems inherent in the original vision. Early design decisions were rethought, and original assumptions were rejected as the light of experience revealed the complexity of the task at hand.

These changes and developments occurred in several areas. The identity of WGU moved from that of a rebellious and impetuous upstart to an institution with modest, if still rather unconventional, ambitions. The competency-based curriculum became more structured and aligned to facilitate student progress. The instructional and advising responsibilities of the institution were recognized and more precisely defined. And WGU adopted a narrower mission in practice, focusing on a niche market in a competitive distance education marketplace.

WGU Identity. The WGU identity was the first to change. In part, this was out of necessity. The amount of time and energy spent promoting the WGU model and explaining it to anyone who would listen was unsustainable

(Kinser, 1999; Meyer, 2005). Between 1996 and 1999, WGU founders, developers, and staff presented updates around the country almost nonstop, in the beginning at the rate of more than one a week (Kinser, 1999). This took time away from the hard tasks of university building. They may have been successful in garnering publicity, but they were less successful in creating a functioning institution. After opening to lackluster enrollment, the staff got off the road and concentrated less on promoting their activities and more on getting things done. The extended development process also made the radical identity of WGU difficult to maintain. The staff recognized this fairly early on. The opening slide of a standard informational presentation began, "Sometimes reputation precedes reality," and attempted to emphasize the careful planning going into this new institution (Kinser, 1999). But the planning, no matter how careful, still was directed at shaking up the status quo.

One problem was accreditation. WGU did not have it, and getting it was anything but simple. The regional accrediting agencies had never approved an institution like WGU before, and they did not immediately accept the model proposed by the governors (Kinser, 2002). The governors, for their part, did not accept the standard accreditation model. They insisted that four regional accreditation agencies—those that had authority over the nineteen participating WGU states—jointly review the institution. As a cross-regional institution, a founding principle of WGU was to break the traditional state-based boundaries of higher education. The governors saw the regional nature of accreditation as part of the problem, and WGU represented its application as an argument for change. The result, however, was that an academic model that would have been difficult enough for one accreditation agency to accept now had to undergo a special review process acceptable to four agencies. Determining whether WGU was eligible for accreditation took three years. Two years later, a decision on candidacy—typically the first step in the accreditation process—was delayed to allow time for the accreditors to better understand the nontraditional nature of the institution (Romboy, 2000). The delay led WGU to apply for national accreditation from DETC (Distance Education and Training Council), apparently deciding that accreditation was too important to hang on principle. As an agency that specializes in distance education, DETC was a much better match for WGU. After just one year, DETC accepted WGU as a fully accredited institution. The regional process continued its slow march forward, ultimately taking nearly seven years for WGU to achieve full accreditation.

The shift to national accreditation is symbolic of the changing WGU identity. Founded to transform traditional higher education, the initial focus was on making a statement about outdated regional accreditation policies. But the policies were robust, and the WGU need for accreditation outweighed the founders' need to make a statement. The path of least resistance was through the DETC. Although this allowed WGU to claim accredited status, it certainly did not represent the gold standard of regional accreditation held by nearly all traditional colleges and universities. It was, in fact, a tacit admission that WGU would not—indeed, could not—force accreditation reform. By 2003, when regional accreditation was finally awarded, the four-agency model was already fading, and the Northwest Commission awarded accreditation on its own authority. Higher education may be resistant to change; WGU could not be.

Curriculum. WGU did not capitulate to traditionalist demands that may have come from its pursuit of regional accreditation. It remains a university that awards degrees based on demonstrated competency rather than the accumulation of course credits. This in itself marks it as a rare departure from most other institutions of higher education. Over the course of its development, however, WGU adjusted the ways in which it accomplished this goal. Originally the plan was to have nearly all elements of the curriculum outsourced to external providers. Now, much is controlled by WGU, and its curriculum is structured in a way that facilitates student completion.

When WGU was founded, the plan for the curriculum was simple: first identify competencies, and then specify the competency assessments. When students take and pass the assessments, they are awarded a WGU degree. The institution took only a passing interest in how students would become competent—perhaps they would take a course at another institution, or maybe just read a book or two—and assumed that assessment of learning would be fairly straightforward. The organization of the curriculum was left to the student, who would be able to decide when and in what order to take the assessments. No semesters or terms were needed, and students would pay for the degree, not the time it took them to complete it. Experience showed, however, that this model was flawed. Revisions began shortly after the first students enrolled.

One key change involved the relationship of the learning resources, competencies, and assessments. The learning resources were originally conceived as a collection of existing courses or programs from third-party providers. Most of the original resources were distance education courses that universities and colleges in participating states had already developed. The connection to competencies was left for the provider to determine, and the WGU catalogue contained many learning resources with little or no relationship to WGU programs. This system became impractical as enrollment increased and the number of learning resources expanded. Now WGU has a much smaller set of providers, most of which are not higher education institutions. Rather than existing courses, WGU more often uses customized programs that are specifically created for WGU students and are directly connected to the competencies. Similarly, WGU was originally committed to using off-the-shelf assessments delivered by third-party providers. This did not work. The assessments could not be consistently developed or delivered to WGU specifications. Now WGU develops all assessments internally and delivers them to students using a secure Internet-based protocol. These two changes allow the learning resource to be aligned with the competencies and the assessment to be aligned with the learning resource. Aside from the obvious curricular benefits of this approach, the process also allows WGU to evaluate the success of each learning resource based on how well students perform on assessments, and use those data to make improvements.

Another change reflects the need for WGU to be able to track student progress better. Although some competency assessments were much more extensive and intense than others, all were originally of equal weight toward the WGU degree. Academic progress was defined as completing a set number of assessments at regular intervals. To connect assessment completion to degree completion better, however, a method of weighting the assessments was needed. WGU established a system of competency units that assigned a number of units to each assessment based on its complexity or difficulty. A simple assessment might be worth one or two competency units, while a more involved assessment could be worth ten or twelve units. Six-month terms were also established, with academic progress measured not by number of assessments but by the number of competency units completed during the term. A personalized academic action plan tells students what learning resources and assessments they should be pursuing during each term. These changes have implications for the financial model of the university as well as its academic model. Rather than being charged by assessment for the degree as a whole, students now pay tuition for each six-month term, which includes all the learning resources and assessments during that term. This not only provides a more regular revenue stream, but by creating a six-month billing cycle, it also creates an incentive for students to move through the program.

A New Faculty Role. From the beginning, WGU had unbundled the faculty role. This meant that discrete activities typically performed by one faculty member in a traditional institution would be handled separately by several different individuals (see Bess and Associates, 2000, for a detailed analysis of the theory behind this idea). WGU did not have faculty in the initial model, and they studiously avoided using that term to describe the individuals who had academic responsibilities. Curricular design and assessment would be covered by various program councils and an assessment council. Full-time WGU staff would advise students on academic requirements. Overall planning would be done by academic officers with terminal degrees in relevant disciplines. And instruction would be the responsibility of outside educational providers, approved by a WGU committee after a review of their education credentials. In the initial design, this mixture of councils and full-time WGU staff serving in planning and advising roles could adequately and appropriately cover all of the traditional faculty functions. Once WGU started enrolling students, however, it became clear that further refinement was necessary.

Some changes represented an extension of the unbundling concept. Graders, for example, were added to take responsibility for evaluating

NEW DIRECTIONS FOR HIGHER EDUCATION • DOI: 10.1002/he

assessments, and additional academic assistance was performed by a group of WGU tutors. This allowed the core student advising responsibility to be handled by mentors. Advisers were added later to support the mentors and handle more routine student interactions that do not require the special skills of the mentors. When the teacher education program was established, a role for coaches—later called clinical supervisors—emerged to support students in field experiences. As WGU grew, these additional roles continued the basic model of differentiating faculty roles.

There was one major departure from the governors' founding vision: WGU established a required course and hired faculty to teach it. A month-long course, Education Without Borders, was established to orient new students to the WGU academic model. This was a significant change for an institution that prided itself on being a nonteaching university and relied on assessments of competencies rather than course completions for a degree. But the varied experiences of students attempting to navigate the unfamiliar WGU model suggested to WGU leaders that they needed to place a requirement for this course into the curriculum. The individuals who teach this course are called facilitators, and they typically are graduates of WGU master's programs who are hired as independent contractors—not, in other words, as members of the regular WGU staff. Facilitators initially also assumed the responsibilities of the tutors, but this role faded in the university and was eventually eliminated. A final instructional role emerged as adjuncts were occasionally named to teach courses designed by nonaccredited education providers. These were hired and supervised by the provider, but naming them WGU adjuncts gave the university control over their qualifications and terms of appointment.

Together, these changes to the faculty role amount to a new recognition of the importance of advising and student support in the nontraditional WGU environment. But they also presage a change in perspective regarding the position of faculty within the institution. WGU clearly demarcates individuals who are considered faculty from those who are not. Mentors are faculty. Advisers are faculty. Members of the program councils are faculty. But graders, facilitators, supervisors, and adjuncts are not. This distinction represents more than a bifurcation of authority. It also suggests how WGU has now embraced the idea of a significant faculty presence within the institution. Early in its existence, WGU was opposed to identifying an individual as a member of the WGU faculty as a matter of principle. But as WGU developed, the term became a useful way of demarking those individuals who have central authority for the curriculum and guiding students through it. At the same time, by applying the faculty label only to certain categories of the traditional faculty role, WGU emphasizes that instruction remains a secondary function in a competency-based university.

Market and Mission. The first degrees developed by WGU were an associate of arts (A.A.) and an associate of applied science in electronics manufacturing technology. The former was intended to serve as the foundation for students transferring into traditional four-year university programs, one of the founding purposes of WGU, while the latter was a response to the technology focus of early corporate supporters. Other two- and four-year technology degrees were added, and a few business degrees rounded out the programs available from WGU at the time of its initial regional accreditation. With the exception of the A.A., these are degrees widely available in the distance education marketplace. Competition was stiff, and WGU's unique competency-based model was a difficult sell. Moreover, other functions that WGU was initially going to perform, such as serving as a clearinghouse and maintaining transcripts for distance education courses, proved to have limited revenue potential. Revenue would have to come from degrees (Meyer, 2005). In short, WGU needed students.

The passage of No Child Left Behind opened up new opportunities for competency-based teacher education. This was not envisioned in the original planning for WGU and represented a transition for the institution. New staff had to be hired to develop the degrees and ensure compatibility with individual state regulations. A graduate degree in learning technology was the first foray, and then a new division was established, WGU Teachers College, that offered teacher certification and graduate degrees at a distance with competencies at the core. The education programs catapulted WGU into a new market, where its programs could gain traction and correspond- ing national prominence. The results were impressive: teacher education now accounts for about three-quarters of WGU's enrollment. This influx of new students in a new program made a big difference for WGU. Two-year degrees were discontinued so the institution could focus on students with higher aspirations—and motivation—associated with four-year and gradu- ate degrees. New degrees were contemplated to take advantage of the national presence that the teacher program had given them. Staffing levels have risen exponentially to keep pace with student enrollment. WGU is a rapidly expanding organization, a far cry from the shaky status it held during the long slog toward accreditation (Kinser, 2002).

One consequence of the teacher education–based expansion is that the mission of the institution has narrowed. Although the broad language of the original mission statement remains unchanged and still represents the institutional ideal, WGU has in practice a mission directed toward serving a niche market. WGU is a distance education institution that focuses on a few well-defined degrees. It competes with other distance education insti- tutions by promoting its distinctive competency-based approach. This means that major online programs and universities such as Capella Univer- sity, Walden University, and the University of Phoenix form its major peer group. The recalcitrant traditional institutions that inspired the governors to create WGU as a catalyst for change are not in the mix. Even as WGU has established a successful program in teacher education that challenges exist- ing programs on traditional campuses across the country, there has been little reaction from the higher education community. There have been no presentations at national meetings and few stories in major newspapers. It is little wonder, then, that WGU dropped off the radar for traditional higher education. WGU is a niche institution now and no longer symbolic of changes threatening higher education.

WGU Success

Innovations usually fail. This is the nature of trying something new: it might not work. Begun as a bold experiment in redesigning postsecondary education, WGU certainly qualifies as a significant attempt at innovation. Almost as certainly, it came close to failing. The barriers to success were substantial. They can be summarized as legitimacy, technology, and money. WGU managed to overcome each.

Legitimacy was the only barrier initially recognized by the governors (Kinser, 2002; Meyer, 2005). A design team dominated by individuals with strong academic credentials knew that they faced an uphill battle for acceptance (see Ashworth, 1996, for an example of how the idea was initially received). Consequently, an enormous amount of energy was spent promoting and defending the WGU concept to academia. A single-minded drive for regional accreditation consumed the design team. Ironically, however, earning accreditation ultimately proved anticlimactic, and most of the public promotion stopped after 2000. Legitimacy was aided by other factors. Distance education became routine between the time WGU was proposed and when it became accredited. The radical rhetoric surrounding its founding became indicative of WGU's history rather than its future. As a niche institution, it was more acceptable to the higher education community, and its relatively small size supports an identity of more modest ambitions. Through mission flexibility and sheer dint of perseverance, WGU outlasted its critics. When finally awarded, regional accreditation was a straightforward seal of approval for what WGU had quietly accomplished.

A second barrier of technology was not recognized by the founders. They assumed that any problems with their plans would come from resistance to technology-based delivery of education, not the underlying mechanics of it. Technological issues, however, proved to be substantial. Initial plans for a distributed organizational architecture were replaced by a geographically centralized administration. Developing and delivering valid and reliable assessments took several years of trial and error before a satisfactory result was achieved. Determining how to support students at a distance and ensure their success in the WGU competency-based curriculum is an ongoing concern. Belief in the power of technology, however naive at WGU's founding, was an unquestioned principle of the institution. The technology could be found to solve almost any problem. When off-the-shelf solutions were inadequate, WGU staff designed their own.

Finally, the barrier of money was anticipated by the governors, but only as a short-term, start-up concern that would be handled by one-time state contributions and corporate partnerships. The extended development time, however, meant that external support from grants and philanthropic donations became the primary source of revenue (Meyer, 2005). It was fortuitous that WGU was founded as a nonprofit institution. There was no need to provide a financial return to investors, and gifts of money and other tangible goods were tax deductible for the contributing corporations. Large federal grants, premised on WGU's politically backed potential, provided a second major source of revenue. The university thus gained time to find its footing. Not until enrollment picked up in 2003, after eight years of going to supporters hat in hand, was WGU able to make the transition to the tuition-supported model that its founders had envisioned.

Each of these barriers demanded that the WGU staff adapt to new circumstances. Trying to build legitimacy by explaining the concept and pushing for regional accreditation had limited effect. So the staff got off the road and took an easier path to accreditation. Assumptions that third-party providers could handle the technology of a competency-based virtual university proved erroneous, so WGU developed the internal capacity to create what was needed. Revenue did not come from the expected sources, so the business plan was revised and other sources of funding pursued. Throughout, however, the central idea of building a competency-based virtual university remained. Modifications to the periphery helped the core innovation survive.

Conclusion

Higher education is littered with examples of innovative institutions and programs that quickly succumbed to the inertia of standard academic practice. But often enough—indeed, more often than many critics of higher education acknowledge—an innovation sticks. As WGU demonstrates, success does not come by tilting at windmills. Change and modification are necessary, but with a constant guard against falling prey to the temptations of tradition. WGU today is different from what the founding governors imagined. The core idea, however, survived a tumultuous beginning, and the institution now operates from a position of strength. The WGU vision is reality.

References

Allen, I. E., and Seaman, J. *Entering the Mainstream: The Quality and Extent of Online Education in the United States, 2003 and 2004.* Needham and Wellesley, Mass.: Sloan Consortium, 2004.
Ashworth, K. H. "Virtual Universities Could Only Produce Virtual Learning." *Chronicle of Higher Education,* Sept. 6, 1996, p. A88.
Bess, J. L., and Associates. *Teaching Alone, Teaching Together: Transforming the Structure of Teams for Teaching.* San Francisco: Jossey-Bass, 2000.
Carnevale, D. "Legislative Audit Criticizes Western Governors University." *Chronicle of Higher Education,* Oct. 6, 2000, p. A48.

Kinser, K. "The Origins, Development and Implications of the Western Governors University." Unpublished doctoral dissertation, Columbia University, 1999.

Kinser, K. "Taking WGU Seriously: Implications of the Western Governors University." *Innovative Higher Education,* 2002, *26*(3), 161–173.

Marchese, T. "Not-So-Distant Competitors: How New Providers Are Remaking the Postsecondary Marketplace." *AAHE Bulletin,* May–June 1998, pp. 3–11.

Meyer, K. A. "Critical Decisions Affecting the Development of Western Governors University." *Innovative Higher Education,* 2005, *30*(5), 177–194.

Romboy, D. "Path to Get Accredited Long, Slow for WGU." *Deseret News,* June 26, 2000, p. A1.

Western Governors Association. *From Vision to Reality.* Denver: Western Governors Association, 1996.

Zemsky, R., and Massey, W. F. *Thwarted Innovation: What Happened to E-learning and Why.* Philadelphia: University of Pennsylvania, 2004.

KEVIN KINSER is an assistant professor in the Department of Educational Administration and Policy Studies at the University of Albany, State University of New York, and a PROPHE Collaborating Scholar.

3

The concepts of the applied universal design movement have created fresh perspectives on management tasks and opportunities.

Universal Design Across the Curriculum

Robbin Zeff

Sometimes an idea emerges out of a confluence of events and moves beyond its original use. The idea of universal design, though originally developed for making the physical environment accessible to the disability community, is one such idea. When applied to higher education, universal design brings a framework for making learning more accessible and instruction more responsive and inclusive to all students.

Universal design entered the scene in the field of architecture and design to make the built world barrier free for the disability community. The concept was developed by architect Ron Mace, who himself was in a wheelchair. Responding to the federal legislation in the 1970s and 1980s calling for public spaces to be accessible to the growing disability community, Mace found that adding accessibility features such as wheelchair ramps to an already built structure detracted from the architectural design and was not as effective as when the building was designed from inception with the most users in mind. Mace also noticed that features included to meet the needs of those with disabilities actually benefited all users. The classic example was curb cuts on sidewalks. Originally mandated for sidewalk wheelchair access, curb cuts quickly became favorites of parents pushing baby strollers, children on skateboards and bicycles, and people pulling luggage on wheels. This design feature added to make sidewalks more accessible to people with disabilities benefited all users.

In the 1980s and early 1990s, the concept of universal design took hold in architecture and design. What emerged were products designed

NEW DIRECTIONS FOR HIGHER EDUCATION, no. 137, Spring 2007 © Wiley Periodicals, Inc.
Published online in Wiley InterScience (www.interscience.wiley.com) • DOI: 10.1002/he.244

and developed for the disability community transitioning to general consumer product status because of superior design (Mace, 1998). For example, wide-handled kitchen utensils, such as wide-handled vegetable peelers developed by OXO Good Grips, were originally designed for use by the founder, Sam Farber, for his wife, Betsey, who had trouble using kitchen tools due to arthritis in her hands (OXO International, 2006). The concept of wide-handled kitchen tools benefited all cooks, making the OXO Good Grips product line a kitchen standard ("Designing for the 21st Century," 2000).

Superior products alone are not what made universal design gain mainstream acceptance in architecture and design. Universal design blossomed out of the confluence of three societal forces: changing demographics (the rising population of people with disabilities whether as the result of war, accident, birth, or aging), federal legislation in response to this changing demographic (Architectural Barriers Act of 1968, Section 504 of the Rehabilitation Act of 1973, Fair Housing Amendments Action of 1988, and Americans with Disabilities Act of 1990), and developments in engineering and technology pushing innovations in the scope of assistive technology: the products that help make the physical world accessible to people with disabilities such as wheelchairs and even prescription glasses (Story, Mueller, and Mace, 1998).

Like universal design in the physical environment, the same types of societal forces are at work today to bring the application and acceptance of universal design to higher education: (1) the pressures of the expanding diversity of today's student population, (2) the social and pedagogical challenges of integrating digital technology into higher education, and (3) political pressures for greater accessibility and the regional accrediting agencies' evolving mandates for outcome assessment.

This chapter looks at five postsecondary universal design initiatives that represent a response to these societal forces. The five initiatives featured represent market leaders in universal design research and application in higher education. In each case, the application of universal design made the transition, as in architecture and design, from the original intention of serving students with disabilities to benefiting all students across the campus.

Pioneers

The father of universal design, Ron Mace, defined the concept as "the design of products and environments to be usable by all people, to the greatest extent possible, without the need for adaptation or specialized design" (Center for Universal Design, 1997) and formulated seven principles governing the concept:

> Principle One: Equitable Use—The design is useful and marketable to people with diverse abilities.

NEW DIRECTIONS FOR HIGHER EDUCATION • DOI: 10.1002/he

Principle Two: Flexibility in Use—The design accommodates a wide range of individual preferences and abilities.

Principle Three: Simple and Intuitive—Use of the design is easy to understand, regardless of the user's experience, knowledge, language skills, or current concentration level.

Principle Four: Perceptible Information—The design communicates necessary information effectively to the user, regardless of ambient conditions or the user's sensory abilities.

Principle Five: Tolerance for Error—The design minimizes hazards and the adverse consequences of accidental or unintended actions.

Principle Six: Low Physical Effort—The design can be used efficiently and comfortably and with a minimum of fatigue.

Principle Seven: Size and Space for Approach and Use—Appropriate size and space is provided for approach, reach, manipulation, and use regardless of user's body size, posture, or mobility [Story, Mueller, and Mace, 1998, pp. 34–35].

These principles, though tied to the physical environment, have as their core keeping as many users in mind as possible in the design and development process. And by so doing, "Universal design provides a blueprint for maximum inclusion of all people" (Story, Mueller, and Mace, 1998, p. 13).

Universal design's application to education has resulted in a veritable alphabet soup of acronyms, from universal design for learning (UDL), to universal instructional design (UID), to universal design for instruction (UDI). Although each institute has reasons for its choice of acronym, the end result is the same: the application of universal design principles to higher education to make teaching and learning accessible to all students.

One of the first groups to apply the idea of universal design to education was CAST (Center for Applied Special Technology), founded in 1984 by hospital-based education researchers and clinicians who were inspired by new computer technologies entering the classroom and wanted to explore how these technologies could be used to assist students with disabilities in primary and secondary schools (Center for Applied Special Technology, 2006a). Impressed by the concept of universal design as applied to architecture, the CAST team saw its immediate applicability to the K–12 educational environment. With expansion of the 1975 Education for Handicapped Children Act (now the Individuals with Disabilities Education Act) guaranteeing public education to children with disabilities, the need for methodologies and theories for teaching students with disabilities expanded dramatically. Applying universal design to the curriculum would mean building courses and classroom activities from inception to meet the learning needs of the greatest number of students, thereby challenging the common practice of pulling children with disabilities out of class for special instruction. CAST realized that what the application of universal

NEW DIRECTIONS FOR HIGHER EDUCATION • DOI: 10.1002/he

design brought to this setting was a recognition and appreciation of flexibility: flexibility in approach, delivery, and application. Moreover, "modifying from inception" in education meant building out curriculum and lessons from a set of goals. CAST named its application of universal design in this context universal design for learning (UDL) and reworked and modified the original seven principles of universal design as defined by Mace to three overarching UDL principles:

> Multiple means of representation—to give learners various ways of acquiring information and knowledge. [This means presenting information in multiple formats from lecture to discussion to individual and group assignments.]
>
> Multiple means of expression—to provide learners alternatives for demonstrating what they know. [This means offering students different pathways for action and expression for demonstrating learning from writing papers, to doing a PowerPoint presentation, to blogging on a topic, and so on.]
>
> Multiple means of engagement—to tap into learners' interests, offer appropriate challenges, and increase motivation. [The addition of UDL does not reduce the rigor of the learning; rather, it recognizes different learning styles, needs, and abilities to allow each learner to capitalize on his other learning strengths.] [Center for Applied Special Technology, 2006b].

Despite coming in to universal design through an interest in assistive technology product design, CAST embraced universal design precisely because of its propensity for making learning accessible to all with or without the aid of technology. Today CAST's mission (2006a) is "to expand learning opportunities for all individuals, especially those with disabilities, through the research and development of innovative, technology-based educational resources and strategies." With a staff of specialists in curriculum development, education policy, neuropsychology, clinical and school psychology, technology, and engineering, CAST is seeding the educational environment with UDL-based solutions. CAST recognized that UDL does not eliminate the need for assistive technology; rather, CAST embraces the power of digital technology in the classroom and the importance of assistive technology's seamless integration into the curriculum so that it becomes merely one of many tools all students may use. From curriculum planning to teacher preparation to software development, CAST is a world leader in the application of UDL in the K–12 classroom. It is equally involved in state and national policymaking in ensuring that the development, distribution, and assessment of digital instructional material meets the National Instructional Material Accessibility Standard.

CAST's primary focus remains K–12 education, but it has expanded its professional development work to higher education. In fact, most of the higher education applications of universal design discussed in this chapter began their projects by examining CAST's work.

Responding to Student Diversity

The first societal force that brought interest in universal design to higher education was the growing number of students with disabilities on college campuses. In 2003–2004, 11 percent of undergraduates reported having a disability, and of them, 40 percent reported having learning disabilities, making it fastest-growing group (Henderson, 2001; Horn and Nevill, 2006). Moreover, just as the number of students with learning disabilities is growing, the entire student population is becoming more diverse. Students today are older, more ethnically diverse, more likely to be nonnative speakers of English, and represent different economic backgrounds (American Council on Education, 2005; Eckel and King, 2004; King, 2006; Paulson and Boeke, 2006; U.S. Department of Education and National Center for Education Statistics, 2006). From addressing the needs of students with disabilities to recognizing the impact of multiculturalism in the classroom, to embracing a wider age range of students, the traditional pedagogies and practices of instruction in higher education are being challenged to make education accessible to a broad range of learners. The examples of the application of universal design in higher education in this chapter demonstrate how this approach seamlessly meets the learning and teaching needs of the expanding diverse student population.

In 1999, Teaching Support Services (TSS) of the University of Guelph in Ontario, Canada, was approached by the Center for Students with Disabilities to develop material for faculty on how to better design their courses to meet the needs of students with disabilities. Because TSS oversaw general faculty development, instructional technology, and instructional design, it looked at the learning needs of students with disabilities and how those needs could be applied to any course. What they found was that the strategies and techniques they were recommending for faculty to implement for students with disabilities actually benefited all students. TSS started researching these findings and stumbled on Frank Bowe's 2000 book, *Universal Design in Education: Teaching Nontraditional Students*. Being from the field of instructional design and using Bowe's book with its reference to universal instructional design (UID), TSS adopted UID as its road map for better and more inclusive instruction (A. Caputo, interview with the author, July 11, 2006).

Because TSS learned about the concept of universal design after it was already applying it intuitively and since its roots were in instructional design, its definition of UID was more directed toward instructional design than the concept's physical environment heritage. As such, the definition of UID put forth by TSS is as follows:

> UID is not just about accessibility for persons with a disability—it's about truly universal thinking—considering the potential needs of all learners when designing and delivering instruction. Through that process, one can identify

and eliminate barriers to teaching and learning, thus maximizing learning for students of all backgrounds and learner preferences, while minimizing the need for special accommodations and maintaining academic rigor [Palmer and Caputo, 2005, p. 1].

TSS began its UID study in 2002 with a grant from the provincial government's Learning Opportunities Task Force. The project began with a series of queries: How can the barriers to success in education be reduced? How can diversity in learning needs and capabilities be the basis for inclusion rather than exclusion? And finally, how would teaching and learning benefit from the application of UID principles (Palmer and Caputo, 2005)? The project then worked with faculty willing to apply UID in their courses by making changes to curriculum, materials, and delivery. As part of the project, they developed comprehensive workbooks for incorporating UID into the design and development of curriculum in face-to-face and distance-learning courses (Teaching Support Services, 2003).

The UID project involved faculty from the sciences, the social sciences, and the humanities. Faculty who fully embraced the UID perspective first assessed the challenges of their individual courses and then applied UID principles in major course redesigns (Teaching Support Services, 2004). For example, a professor who teaches the large first-year chemistry course found that the students had a tendency to memorize rather than learn course concepts. The UID project redesigned the course to have a problem-solving approach through learning and instructional media. A French professor identified that students who studied French lacked a basic knowledge of French literature and culture. In response, the UID project developed a self-directed tutorial game where the main character grows in sophistication as the player progresses through the game. And a professor of an upper-level nutrition course that covers highly technical material wanted to include more active learning strategies rather than presentation lectures, thereby better aligning the course objectives with the course content. The UID project redesigned all the course material, developed Web-based resources, and designed classroom activities for more active learning.

At the same time the University of Guelph was beginning its work on making courses more accessible to students with disabilities, a team of faculty at the Center on Postsecondary Education and Disability (CPED) at the University of Connecticut was also working on the application of universal design to higher education. Recognizing the diversity in the student body in terms of students with disabilities as well as ethnic and age diversity, CPED wanted to build a theory around the concept of universal design that would aid faculty in teaching this diverse student body (McGuire, Scott, and Shaw, 2003).

The team of Joan McGuire, Sally Scott, and Stan Shaw coined the term *universal design for instruction* because they felt that what they were doing was an offshoot of universal design applied to instruction and not instructional design made universal (J. Scott, interview with the author, July 21, 2006). In other words, they applied the theory of universal design to classroom instruction as ". . . an approach to teaching that consists of the proactive design and use of inclusive instructional strategies that benefit a broad range of learners including students with disabilities" (Scott, McGuire, and Embry, 2002).

When they began their work in 1999, they looked at all who were applying universal design to education (Scott, McGuire, and Foley, 2003). They looked at what CAST was doing, but found that its three principles were not comprehensive enough for the theoretical perspective they sought to establish. They went back to the original seven principles of universal design and reworked them to fit a higher education frame. They also looked at Chickering and Gamson's classic, "Seven Principles for Good Practice in Undergraduate Education" (1987). The result was a list of nine principles for UDI (McGuire, Scott, and Shaw, 2003, p. 13):

1. Equitable use—Instruction is designed to be useful to and accessible by people with diverse abilities. Provide the same means of use for all students, identical whenever possible, equivalent when not. [Example: Using web-based courseware products with links to on-line resources so all students can access materials, regardless of varying academic preparation, distance from campus, etc.]

2. Flexibility in use—Instruction is designed to accommodate a wide range of individual abilities. Provide choice in methods of use. [Example: Using varied instructional methods (lecture with a visual outline, group activities, use of stories, or web-based discussions) to support different ways of learning.]

3. Simple and intuitive instruction—Instruction is designed in a straightforward and predictable manner, regardless of the student's experience, knowledge, language skills, or current concentration level. Eliminate unnecessary complexity. [Example: Providing a grading scheme for papers or projects to clearly state performance expectations.]

4. Perceptible information—Instruction is designed so that necessary information is communicated effectively, regardless of ambient conditions or the student's sensory abilities. [Example: Selecting text books, reading material, and other instructional supports in digital format so students with diverse needs can access materials through print or by using technological supports (e.g., screen reader, text enlarger).]

5. Tolerance for error—Instruction anticipates variation in individual student learning pace and prerequisite skills. [Example: Structuring a long-term course project with the option of turning in individual project components separately for constructive feedback and for integration into the final product.]

6. Low physical effort—Instruction is designed to minimize nonessential physical effort in order to allow maximum attention to learning. Note: This

principle does not apply when physical effort is integral to essential requirements of a course. [Example: Allowing students to use a word processor for writing and editing papers or essay exams.]

7. Size and space for approach and use—Instruction is designed with consideration for appropriate size and space for approach, reach, manipulations, and use regardless of a student's body size, posture, mobility, and communication needs. [Example: Using a circular seating arrangement in small class settings to allow students to see and face speakers during discussion—important for students with attention problems.]

8. A community of learners—The instructional environment promotes interaction and communication among students and between students and faculty. [Example: Fostering communication among students in and out of class by structuring study and discussion groups, e-mail lists, or chat rooms.]

9. Instructional climate—Instruction is designed to be welcoming and inclusive. High expectations are espoused for all students. [Example: Creating a statement on the syllabus affirming the need for students to respect diversity, underscoring the expectation of tolerance, and encouraging students to discuss any special learning needs with the instructor] [Shaw, Scott, and McGuire, Nov. 2001].

The program conducted research with the key constituent groups of students, faculty, and disability service professionals to explore the applicability and acceptability of UDI in postsecondary education within and outside the disability milieu (Scott and McGuire, 2005). The result was a focus on using faculty development, not only because that was the purpose of the funding, but also because of their respect for faculty and their desire to harness the natural intellectual curiosity of academic faculty and channel it into asking questions about UDI (J. McGuire, interview with the author, July 21, 2006). They used faculty development as a means of introducing UDI into the college classroom with the goal of changing faculty behavior and improving student learning. Equally important, they made sure they did not make one discipline dominant in their research; instead, they developed a theory-based perspective that targeted the teacher, not the discipline (S. Scott, interview with the author, July 5, 2006). In other words, they integrated universal design into all curriculum, and in so doing, showed how UDI helped faculty improve their courses to meet the needs of all students.

Expanding Role of Technology

The second societal force is the expanding role of technology in education today. In fact, the promise and potential of technology in the classroom is an old discussion. For the past fifteen years, technology has been touted as having tremendous potential for improving education. Without a doubt, through the 1990s and early 2000, the broad application of the Internet and the rush to find applications of value received unparalleled hype. Without a doubt, merely transferring existing teaching and pedagogical practices to a digital dimension failed to use the technological tools—whether word processing, presentation, or course management software—to their fullest potential. Studies have shown that when technology replicated a lecture format of instruction, whether the technology was radio, television, or online, there was no significant difference in learning (Howell, 2001). And yet, just as Yale University professor of information design Edward Tufte (2003) criticizes PowerPoint® for the limitations it puts on creativity and information presentation, Tufte's critics point out that one cannot blame the product because of the failings of its users (Doumont, 2005; Simons, 2004). Today technological applications and accessibility have finally caught up to the potential of technology by using it for more than merely replicating a lecture setting. Integrated approaches where the curriculum is redesigned to marry good pedagogy with appropriate uses of technology are not only improving the quality of education but reducing costs as well (Graves and Twigg, 2006; Spelling Commission on the Future of Higher Education, 2006).

These developments are crucial because today's students have grown up with computers and the Internet. In fact, students today do not know life without instant messaging, text messaging, and downloadable music. With 70 percent Internet penetration in the U.S. population and home broadband use of the Internet at 30 percent and climbing steadily, digital technology is now as accessible and pervasive in the home as other forms of communication (Horrigan, 2006a, 2006b). The pervasiveness of technology on college campuses today can be summed up in the findings from the spring 2006 *Student Monitor* that found iPods were more popular than beer (Associated Press, 2006; Snider, 2006). The only other time beer lost its preeminence on the survey was when it was preempted in 1997 by the Internet itself. Facebook (not even ranked in 2005) was number 3, text messaging was number 5, and MySpace was 13.

Like CAST, a team at the University of Washington's Adaptive Technology Lab, under the leadership of Sheryl Burgstahler, started exploring the uses of computer technology in the classroom in 1984. In 1999 they received a grant from the Office of Postsecondary Education as part of its Demonstration Projects to Ensure Quality Higher Education for Students with Disabilities to establish DO-IT (Disabilities Opportunities, Internetworking, and Technology) to research and design faculty development material on how to better meet the needs of students with disabilities in the classroom using assistive technology (Burgstahler, n.d. b). The grant resulted in the establishment of The Faculty Room Web site (http://www.washington.edu/doit/Faculty) with its resource material and handouts for faculty on how to work with students with different types of disabilities from a universal design perspective. The researchers received a second grant in 2002 to expand their work in universal design and explore its application to student services and administration. This resulted in the addition of The Conference Room (www.washington.edu/doit/Conf) for staff and administrators at postsecondary institutions with information on how to create accessible facilities, services, and resources and The Board Room (www.washington.edu/doit/Board) for high-level administrators. They received an unprecedented third grant in 2005 to expand how the principles of universal design could be applied across the entire campus (Burgstahler, n.d. a).

As applied by DO-IT, universal design does not eliminate the need for accommodations. Rather, part of universal design is making sure the planning for accommodations is built in, with the application of universal design a thought process and product. According to Burgstahler, one needs to look at universal design's application on both a micro and macro level in instruction (Burgstahler, n.d. b). The macro level is applying it to all teaching. This involves evaluating the learning goals and objectives of a course and applying the right method of teaching for each goal, whether that involves determining how to make a lecture accessible to all students, providing handouts, or not standing with one's back to the students while writing on the board. The micro level would include deciding how to distribute the lecture material, such as having it available in multiple formats on the course Web site and making sure the Web site itself is accessible.

The debate about whether technology has a role in the classroom is over. Technology's pervasiveness in all aspects of life cannot be denied. The challenge that remains is how its application is going to be used and what barriers exist that may hamper innovative educational users of technology (McGeveran and Fisher, 2006). And just as technology alone is not the answer, Burgstahler acknowledges that "universal design is an aspect of good teaching. But universal design alone does not guarantee good teaching" (Burgstahler, n.d. b). Universal design is a strategy that aids in making learning more accessible to all learners through the use of technology.

Political and Assessment Pressures

The pressure for more strategic and comprehensive use of technology and innovative teaching practices is the third societal force and is hitting higher education from all sides. Indeed, one of the few recommendations from the 2006 Secretary of Education's Commission on Higher Education report that did not deal with finances challenged higher education to "embrace a culture of continuous innovation and quality improvement by developing new pedagogies, curricula, and technologies to improve learning . . ." (Spelling Commission on the Future of Higher Education, 2006). And yet turning the call for change into a culture of change is a tall order.

In 1999, five top-ranked institutions (Brown University, Columbia University, Dartmouth College, Harvard University, and Stanford University) joined forces to explore how best to train faculty to more effectively teach students with invisible disabilities on their campuses (Ivy Access Initiative, 2002a). Funded by a grant from the U.S. Department of Education, Office of Postsecondary Education, the Ivy Access Initiative began by gathering information from the key stakeholder groups of students, faculty, and administrators on all five campuses. Through findings from focus groups, surveys, and interviews, a series of workshops for faculty and graduate students was developed on UID. To motivate faculty to apply UID in their courses, faculty development grants were awarded as well.

The project directors purposely did not emphasize the role of technology in universal design because they felt that faculty would find the ideas of UID more accessible if the options focused less on technology and more on modifications in teaching style for individual courses (R. Shaw, interview with the author, June 27, 2006). Faculty applied UID in the courses from modifications in lesson delivery to complete overhauls in teaching style and curriculum (Ivy Access Initiative, 2002b). For example, a computer science professor who had received criticism from his students for not providing enough contextual background for his lectures started opening his lectures with an overview of key concepts and their importance. A psychology professor added flexibility in the execution of his final exam by offering students the option of a take-home or an in-class exam. And a math/statistics faculty member started distributing copies of overheads to the entire class so that students could use them for reference and review. He also began to deliver his lectures with a greater focus on his audience. The changes he made included making eye contact with students, pausing when appropriate, and being more specific in his descriptions.

Universal design's use and applicability to higher education for both faculty and administrators was directly addressed by a team at Ohio State University (OSU), which received a partnership grant from the U.S. Department of Education to study and develop material on improving the quality of higher education for students with disabilities. The first part of the project, which ran from 1999 through 2002, consisted of a climate assessment to identify faculty and administration needs to better serve students with disabilities. The project resulted in the development of a series, "Fast Facts for Faculty," on working with students with disabilities (Ohio State University Partnership Grant, 2000).

The study also identified universal design as the preferred training topic (Izzo and Murray, 2003). As a result, the second part of the project, which ran from 2002 through 2006, focused on creating a faculty development tool on universal design with the following objectives:

- To serve as a professional development resource for faculty, administrators, students, and disability service providers based on identified training needs
- To infuse existing and innovative technologies into models of faculty training

- To provide an anytime, anywhere flexible training medium faculty could access from home or office
- To provide users a customized experience based on existing knowledge (Torres and Scarpino, 2006)

In addition to OSU, there were four national piloting partners (Columbus State Community College, George Washington University, Lansing Community College, and West Chester University) and twenty-three other institutions involved in the project. The project resulted in the development of the Web-based self-paced and interactive training module FAME (Faculty and Administrator Modules in Higher Education) to instruct faculty and administrators on core aspects of servicing the increasing population of students with disabilities on college campuses.

FAME consists of five modules:

- Rights and Responsibilities
- Universal Design for Learning
- Web Accessibility
- College Writing
- Climate Assessment

The modules not only explained universal design's place in higher education and serving students with disabilities, but also demonstrated universal design's application in information delivery through the module's multimodal design. The modules were completed in 2006, and the original intention was to have them available as an online course that resulted in a professional development training certificate for faculty and administrators on better serving students with disabilities on college campuses through the application of universal design. Due to lack of funding, the finished product was never brought to full implementation as a certification source. In June 2006 FAME moved from being housed and maintained by the University of Ohio to its new home on the Ohio Learning Network, an e-learning site that aggregates services for the citizens of Ohio (http://www.oln.org/teaching_and_learning/ada/Fame/FAME_Content/index.html) (M. Izzo, interview with the author, June 7, 2006).

Challenges and Implications

The late Patricia Silver of the University of Massachusetts at Amherst was one of the first to consider universal design in higher education and one of the most forthright in acknowledging the challenges facing its broad adoption by faculty (Silver, 2002; Silver, Bourke, and Strehorn, 1998). In a 2002 piece, she pointed out that not only do faculty have time constraints that hamper the adoption of new teaching techniques and technologies, but they also are reluctant to invest time in course redesign when tenure and promotion decisions are tied more to research than teaching and curriculum development. But even more than that, she recognized that "university settings have traditionally been resistant to change" (p. 1).

The CPED team at the University of Connecticut tried to harness the intellectual curiosity of faculty by basing their UDI work on both research and theory. They not only developed practical tools for UDI's application in course development and delivery, but invested time in extensive academic publishing on UDI in both postsecondary disability journals and more general education journals (McGuire, Scott, and Shaw, 2003, 2006; Scott and McGuire, 2005; Scott, McGuire, and Foley, 2003; Shaw, Scott and McGuire, 2001). Their interest in documenting and demonstrating UDI's fundamental improvement of all dimensions of instruction even led them to do studies on good teaching to see its connection to UDI. The CPED team did a study of how outstanding faculty worked with students with disabilities in their courses and discovered that great teachers were often applying universal design principles without even knowing about universal design (Madaus, Scott, and McGuire, 2003).

Part of the focus of the Ivy Initiative as a faculty development program was to explore how best to bring about change in the instructional culture of postsecondary institutions. The two major findings suggest that the impetus rests at the administrative level (R. Shaw, interview with the author, June 27, 2006). First, the program needs to be promoted by someone who is in a position of authority and has the respect of the faculty. Because the point person at Brown was also the dean of the college, the initiative received greater and more long-lasting attention than at the other campuses. And second, for that change to occur, there needed to be an ambassador promoting instructional change in each department, because the audience for the initiative consisted of faculty at high-profile research institutions where teaching skills are not as highly rewarded as research.

The University of Guelph's UID project included a strong assessment component to evaluate the learning outcomes as well as the instructional applications (Yuval, Procter, Korabik, and Palmer, 2004). Specific findings showed that:

- Application of UID principles created an environment beneficial to students with learning disabilities.
- Students reported significant attitude improvement in learning success.
- Faculty reported significant improvement in student performance (Teaching Support Services, n.d.).

Indeed, their research concluded that the implementation of UID improved student learning and performance.

Unfortunately, in all the case studies presented in this chapter, the material was developed and applied while the funding was ample; not unexpectedly, the institutional buy-in and enthusiasm waned when funding concluded. And yet at each institution, the legacy continues through Web sites and downloadable resources. CAST has an informative Web site and even makes some of its books, such as the highly acclaimed *Teaching Every Student in the Digital Age: Universal Design for Learning*, downloadable for free (http://www.cast.org/teachingeverystudent/ideas/tes/). The team at the University of Connecticut established the FacultyWare Web site (http://www.facultyware.uconn.edu/home.cfm) to educate faculty on UDI, provide resources on UDI and its application in higher education, and provide a venue where applications of UDI could be showcased in a peer-reviewed environment. The continued legacy for the Ivy Initiative primarily rests on its companion Web site (http://www.brown.edu/Administration/Dean_of_the_College/uid), which continues to be updated. One of the most interesting tools on the site is its interactive UID quiz (http://www.brown.edu/Administration/Dean_of_the_College/uid/html/test.shtml).

The funding ended for the University of Guelph's UID project in 2005, but the legacy continues through its online resources (http://www.tss.uoguelph.ca/uid/index.cfm). The University of Guelph's work on UID is now receiving renewed interest from external sources. Following in the footsteps of the Americans with Disabilities Act, the Accessibility for Ontarians with Disabilities Act passed in 2005, requiring that the physical and learning environment be more accessible for Canada's disability community ("New Accessibility Law Now in Effect," 2005).

Conclusion

In this age of outside pressures on higher education (Spelling Commission on the Future of Higher Education, 2006) and calls for increased accountability (Carey, 2006), it is important that higher education take charge of these changes rather than have them placed on it. Without a doubt, "Legislation is a lousy instructional design tool," Scott and McGuire (2003) noted in their PowerPoint® presentation on understanding faculty culture in relation to the adoption of UDI (Scott and McGuire, 2003, slide 5). And although disability law and federal education legislation are not as prescriptive at the college level as K–12, there are forces at work that could change that (Spelling Commission on the Future of Higher Education, 2006).

Universal design as applied to higher education is distinguishing itself as a paradigm capable of meeting the needs of all learners, as well as those who assess learning both inside and outside the academy. Already we are seeing universal design being applied in postsecondary education in fields as diverse as composition and social work (Lightfoot and Gibson, 2005; McAlexander, 2004). Universal design is also being used to rethink test design and delivery (Dolan and others, 2005). And finally, universal design is being applied to large-scale assessments (Bremer, 2004; Thompson, Johnstone, and Thurlow, 2002). In fact, taking its direction from how the original principles of universal design have been reworked for instruction, the assessment community has done the same and come up with its own elements of universally designed assessments (Thompson, Johnstone, and Thurlow, 2002):

- Inclusive assessment population
- Precisely defined constructs
- Accessible, nonbiased items
- Amenable to accommodations
- Simple, clear, and intuitive instructions and procedures
- Maximum readability and comprehensibility
- Maximum legibility

The purpose of these elements when applied to assessment is not merely to make it accessible but to make it authentic, accurate, and authoritative for a student population that is constantly growing in diversity.

Burgstahler and her DO-IT team at the University of Washington see universal design as a concept applicable to all functions of university life: academic and administrative (Burgstahler, n.d. a). Their initial foray into universal design was making computers on campus accessible for students with disabilities in terms of software and hardware and called this practice universal design of information technology. They then focused on classroom instruction, working with faculty to make course design and materials as accessible as possible to all students, and titled this practice universal design of curriculum and instruction. And finally, they explored what universal design could bring to student services from the library to the career center and dubbed this universal design of student services. DO-IT's work demonstrates that universal design is needed not only in all aspects of learning and instruction, but in every touch point in higher education. Perhaps the previous work in universal design in higher education has focused too narrowly on instruction. The path to fuller adoption and implementation should traverse the entire campus.

References

American Council on Education. *College Students Today—A National Portrait.* Washington, D.C.: American Council on Education, 2005.

Associated Press. "iPod Beats Beer in College Popularity Survey." *MacNewsWorld,* June 8, 2006. Retrieved June 26, 2006, from http://gizmodo.com/gadgets/portable-media/ipod-beats-out-beer-in-a-popularity-contest-179296.php.

Bowe, F. G. *Universal Design in Education: Teaching Nontraditional Students.* Westport, Conn.: Bergin Garvey/Greenwood, 2000.

Bremer, C. D. "Universal Design in Secondary and Postsecondary Education." *Impact: Feature Issue on Achieving Secondary Education and Transition Results for Students with Disabilities,* 2004, *16*(3). Retrieved June 25, 2006, from http://ici.umn.edu/products/impact/163/over3.html.

Burgstahler, S. "Applications of Universal Design." *DO-IT.* n.d. a. Retrieved Sept. 4, 2006, from http://www.washington.edu/doit/Resources/udesign.html.

Burgstahler, S. "DO-IT Programs and Resources." *DO-IT.* n.d. b. Retrieved Sept. 4, 2006, from http://www.washington.edu/doit/Programs.

Carey, K. "Is Our Students Learning? The Measurements Elite Colleges Don't Want You to See." *Washington Monthly,* Sept. 2006. Retrieved Sept. 1, 2006, from http://www.washingtonmonthly.com/features/2006/0609.carey.html.

CAST. *History.* 2006a. Retrieved July 5, 2006, from http://www.cast.org/about/history/index.html.

CAST. *What Is Universal Design for Learning?* 2006b. Retrieved Sept. 3, 2006, from http://www.cast.org/research/udl/index.html.

Center for Universal Design. *About Universal Design.* 1997. Retrieved Aug. 9, 2006, from http://www.design.ncsu.edu/cud/about_ud/about_ud.htm.

Chickering, A. W., and Gamson, Z. F. "Seven Principles for Good Practice in Undergraduate Education." *AAHE Bulletin,* Oct. 1987, pp. 3–6.

"Designing for the 21st Century: An International Conference on Universal Design, June 14–18, 2000." *Global Universal Design Educators Monthly Online News,* 2000, 6(2). Retrieved July 5, 2006, from http://www.universaldesign.net/news/jun00.htm.

Dolan, R., and others. "Applying Principles of Universal Design to Test Delivery: The Effect of Computer-Based Read-Aloud on Test Performance of High School Students with Learning Disabilities." *Journal of Technology, Learning, and Assessment,* 2005, 7. Retrieved Sept. 1, 2006, from http://escholarship.bc.edu/jtla/vol3/7/.

Doumont, J. "The Cognitive Style of PowerPoint: Slides Are Not All Evil." *Technical Communication,* 2005, 1, 64–70.

Eckel, P. D., and King, J. E. *An Overview of Higher Education in the United States: Diversity, Access, and the Role of the Marketplace.* Washington, D.C.: American Council on Education, 2004.

Graves, W. H., and Twigg, C. A. "The Future of Course Redesign and the National Center for Academic Transformation: An Interview with Carol A. Twigg." *Innovate,* 2006, 3. Retrieved Aug. 7, 2006, from http://www.innovateonline.info/index.php?view=article&id=218.

Henderson, C. *2001 College Freshman with Disabilities: A Biennial Statistical Profile.* Washington, D.C.: Heath Resource Center, 2001.

Horn, L., and Nevill, S. *Profile of Undergraduates in U.S. Postsecondary Education Institutions: 2003–2004: With a Special Analysis of Community College Students.* Washington, D.C.: National Center for Education Statistics, 2006.

Horrigan, J. *Online News: For Many Home Broadband Users, the Internet Is a Primary News Source.* Washington, D.C.: Pew Internet and American Life Project, 2006a.

Horrigan, J. *Home Broadband Adoption 2006: Home Broadband Adoption Is Going Mainstream and That Means User-Generated Content Is Coming from All Kinds of Internet Users.* Washington, D.C.: Pew Internet and American Life Project, 2006b.

Howell, D. "Elements of Effective E-Learning." *College Teaching,* 2001, 49(3). Retrieved June 18, 2006, from http://www.ebscohost.com.

Ivy Access Initiative. "About the Ivy Access Initiative." *Ivy Access Initiative.* 2002a. Retrieved June 24, 2006, from http://www.brown.edu/Administration/Dean_of_the_College/uid/html/about.shtml.

Ivy Access Initiative. "How Faculty Have Applied Universal Instructional Design in Their Classes." *Ivy Access Initiative.* 2002b. Retrieved June 24, 2006, from http://www.brown.edu/Administration/Dean_of_the_College/uid/html/what_applied.shtml.

Izzo, M., and Murray, A. "Applying Universal Design for Learning Principles to Enhance Achievement of College Students." In S. Acker and C. Gynns (eds.), *Learning Objects: Context and Connections.* Columbus: Ohio State University, 2003. Retrieved June 7, 2006, from http://telr-research.osu.edu/learning_objects/index.html.

King, J. E. *Working Their Way Through College: Student Employment and Its Impact on the College Experience.* Washington, D.C.: American Council on Education, 2006.

Lightfoot, E., and Gibson, P. "Universal Instructional Design: A New Framework for Accommodating Students in Social Work Courses." *Journal of Social Work Education,* 2005, *41,* 269–277.

Mace, R. "A Perspective on Universal Design." Paper presented at Designing for the 21st Century: An International Conference on Universal Design, June 19, 1998, Boston, MA. Retrieved June 25, 2006, from http://www.adaptenv.org/index.php?option=Resource&articleid=156.

Madaus, J. W., Scott, S., and McGuire, J. *Addressing Student Diversity in the Classroom: The Approaches of Outstanding University Professors.* Storrs: Center on Postsecondary Education and Disability, University of Connecticut, 2003. Retrieved July 5, 2006, from http://www.facultyware.uconn.edu/TechnicalReports.cfm.

McAlexander, P. "Using Principles of Universal Design in College Composition Courses: Review of Reviewed Item." *Basic Writing e-Journal,* 2004, *1.* Retrieved Jan. 11, 2006, from http://www.asu.edu/clas/english/composition/cbw/BWEspring2004.html.

McGeveran, W., and Fisher, W. W. *The Digital Learning Challenge: Obstacles to Educational Uses of Copyrighted Material in the Digital Age.* Cambridge, Mass.: Berkman Center, Aug. 2006. Retrieved Aug. 30, 2006, from http://ssrn/abstract=923465.

McGuire, J. M., Scott, S. S., and Shaw, S. F. "Universal Design for Instruction: The Paradigm, Its Principles, and Products for Enhancing Instructional Access." *Journal of Postsecondary Education and Disability,* 2003, *17,* 11–21.

McGuire, J. M., Scott, S. S., and Shaw, S. F. "Universal Design and Its Applications in Educational Environments." *Remedial and Special Education,* 2006, *27,* 166–175.

"New Accessibility Law Now in Effect: Accessibility for Ontarians with Disabilities Act, 2005 Receives Royal Assent." News release. 2005. Retrieved July 11, 2006, from http://www.citizenship.gov.on.ca/english/about/n140605.htm.

Ohio State University Partnership Grant. *Fast Facts for Faculty Series.* 2000. Retrieved June 26, 2006, from http://www.osu.edu/grants/dpg/fastfact/index.html.

OXO International. "Our Roots." *OXO,* 2006. Retrieved Sept. 3, 2006, from http://www.oxo.com/oxo/about_roots.htm.

Palmer, J., and Caputo, A. *The Universal Instructional Design Implementation Guide.* Ontario: University of Guelph, 2005. Retrieved June 19, 2006, from http://www.tss.uoguelph.ca/uid/uid-implementation-guide-v4.pdf.

Paulson, K., and Boeke, M. *Adult Learners in the United States: A National Profile.* Washington, D.C.: American Council on Education, 2006.

Scott, S. S., and McGuire, J. M. *Collaborating with Faculty in an Era of Universal Design for Instruction: Update on UDI: Understanding Faculty Culture.* 2003. Retrieved July 5, 2006, from http://vm.uconn.edu/~wwwcped/sm-day1.pdf.

Scott, S. S., and McGuire, J. M. *Universal Design for Instruction: A Demonstration Project at the University of Connecticut.* 2005. Retrieved June 26, 2006, from http://www.facultyware.uconn.edu/files/UDIProjectOverviewFW.doc.

Scott, S. S., McGuire, J. M., and Embry, P. *Universal Design for Instruction Fact Sheet.* 2002. Retrieved June 26, 2006, from http://www.facultyware.uconn.edu/udi_factsheet.cfm.

Scott, S. S., McGuire, J. M., and Foley, T. E. "Universal Design for Instruction: A Framework for Anticipating and Responding to Disability and Other Diverse Learning Needs in the College Classroom." *Equity and Excellence in Education,* 2003, *36,* 40–49.

Shaw, S. F., Scott, S. S., and McGuire, J. M. *Teaching College Students with Learning Disabilities.* Arlington, Va.: Council for Exceptional Children, 2001.

Silver, P. "The Challenge of Implementing Universal Instructional Design in Higher Education." *Ivy Access Initiative,* 2002. Retrieved June 24, 2006, from http://www.brown.edu/Administration/Dean_of_the_College/uid/docs/challenge.pdf.

Silver, P., Bourke, A., and Strehorn, K. C. "Universal Instructional Design in Higher Education: An Approach for Inclusion." *Equity and Excellence in Education*, 1998, *31*, 47–51.

Simons, T. "Does PowerPoint Make You Stupid?" *Presentations*, Apr. 7, 2004. Retrieved July 17, 2006, from www.sociablemedia.com/PDF/press_presentations_magazine_03_01_04.pdf.

Snider, M. "iPods Knock Over Beer Mugs; College Kids Rank What's Most Popular." *USA Today*, June 8, 2006. Retrieved June 26, 2006, from http://www.usatoday.com/tech/news/2006-06-07-ipod-tops-beer_x.htm.

Spelling Commission on the Future of Higher Education. *A National Dialogue: The Secretary of Education's Commission on the Future of Higher Education*. Washington, D.C.: Department of Education, 2006. Retrieved Sept. 1, 2006, from http://www.ed.gov/about/bdscomm/list/hiedfuture/reports.html.

Story, M. F., Mueller, J. L., and Mace, R. L. *The Universal Design File: Designing for People of All Ages and Abilities*. Raleigh: Center for Universal Design, North Carolina State University, 1998. Retrieved June 25, 2006, from http://design.ncsu.edu/cud/pubs_p/pudfiletoc.htm.

Teaching Support Services. *A Workbook for Faculty Teaching at a Distance*. Ontario: University of Guelph, 2003. Retrieved June 26, 2006, from http://www.tss.uoguelph.ca/uid/uid-workbook-DE.pdf.

Teaching Support Services. *UID Case Studies*. Ontario: University of Guelph, 2004. Retrieved June 26, 2006, from http://www.tss.uoguelph.ca/uid/uidcasestudies.cfm.

Teaching Support Services. *UID Summary*. Ontario: University of Guelph, n.d. Retrieved June 26, 2006, from http://www.tss.uoguelph.ca/uid/uidsummary.cfm.

Thompson, S. J., Johnstone, C. J., and Thurlow, M. L. *Universal Design Applied to Large Scale Assessments*. Minneapolis: University of Minnesota, National Center on Educational Outcomes, 2002. Retrieved June 25, 2006, from http://education.umn.edu/NCEO/OnlinePubs/Synthesis44.html.

Torres, K., and Scarpino, A. "Universal Design for Learning (UDL) and College Writing: Faculty and Administrator Modules (FAME) in Higher Education." Presentation at the CCCC Annual Convention, Chicago, 2006.

Tufte, E. R. *The Cognitive Style of PowerPoint*. Cheshire, Conn.: Graphics Press, 2003.

U.S. Department of Education, and National Center for Education Statistics. *The Condition of Education 2006*. Washington, D.C.: U.S. Government Printing Office, 2006.

Yuval, L., Procter, E., Korabik, K., and Palmer, J. *Evaluation Report on the Universal Instructional Design Project at the University of Guelph*. Ontario: University of Guelph, 2004.

ROBBIN ZEFF is an assistant professor of writing and professional technology fellow in the University Writing Program at The George Washington University.

4

Creating a new generation of leaders and managers has been the task of the innovative U.K. Leadership Foundation for Higher Education.

A Challenging Journey: From Leadership Courses to Leadership Foundation for Higher Education

Robin Middlehurst

In 1978, John Adair was appointed professor of leadership studies at the University of Surrey in the United Kingdom. His was a landmark appointment in two ways. First, this chair was the first professorial-level appointment in leadership studies in the world, and second, Adair's appointment sparked a range of leadership development initiatives in higher education, from leadership courses for students, new graduates, and alumni to programs for departmental chairs and more senior academic and administrative staff. Prior to the 1980s, academic staff training had largely focused on the development of teachers and teaching (Matheson, 1981).

Over two decades, and building on Adair's pioneering work, colleagues of Adair (alongside others) have sought to develop and tailor leadership and management programs to the specific context of universities, drawing on parallel research efforts. Since the late 1980s and early 1990s, initiatives in management and leadership development have spread, albeit unevenly, across higher education in the United Kingdom. However, the research base has not grown commensurately. By 2000, it was clear that higher education still lagged behind other sectors (such as health, industry, or local government) in its attention to management and leadership development and research on the running of the business. The sector also trailed its major competitor, the United States, which had established a national lead in leadership development through the work of the American Council on Education (Green and McDade, 1991).

NEW DIRECTIONS FOR HIGHER EDUCATION, no. 137, Spring 2007   © Wiley Periodicals, Inc.
Published online in Wiley InterScience (www.interscience.wiley.com) • DOI: 10.1002/he.245

The picture changed in a significant way in 2003–2004. Acting on research findings, a changing political climate, and awareness of increasing economic, social, and political challenges for institutions, the higher education funding bodies in England, Scotland, Wales, and Northern Ireland made a significant investment in leadership development. With collective ownership by higher education's representative bodies (Universities UK and the Standing Conference of Principals) and start-up funding from the councils, the Leadership Foundation for Higher Education was established. This chapter discusses this innovation, tracing its roots back to the research and development work in the United Kingdom that lies behind it. The chapter also highlights the challenges that surround the topic of leadership development in higher education. There are three parts to the story: putting leadership development on the map; moving the agenda forward—research, politics, and timing; and the Leadership Foundation in action—challenges and opportunities.

Although this chapter focuses on one national initiative, the context will be familiar to other countries where higher education reforms call for strengthened leadership, management, and governance as part of the balance between increased autonomy and accountability for institutions (World Bank, 2002). The initiative was also developed in the light of comparisons with other sectors and countries, particularly the United States, but also Canada, Australia, South Africa, and continental Europe. Both the journey taken and the model adopted for the foundation should be of interest beyond the United Kingdom.

Putting Leadership Development on the Map in Higher Education

Based on early analysis and development of leadership training for the army and subsequent work with commerce and industry, John Adair developed a model of leadership known as functional or action-centered leadership (Adair, 1968). He was influenced by American work on group dynamics and motivation (Lewin, 1944; Maslow, 1954) as well as the work of early management theorists, such as Fayol (1949). Adair proposed that people in working groups—whether small teams or large organizations—had three sets of needs that had to be fulfilled if performance and satisfaction were to be achieved. These he illustrated in terms of three overlapping circles: a need to achieve a common task, to be kept together as a working group, and to achieve individual motivation, development, and satisfaction (see Figure 4.1). The function of leadership, exercised through the actions and behaviors of leaders who carried the leadership role, was to ensure that these three sets of needs were met and kept in balance. Adair also identified a number of functional responsibilities for leaders in relation to each circle (setting objectives, briefing, planning, controlling, informing, supporting, and reviewing). His success criteria for leadership revolved around direction setting, achievement

Figure 4.1. John Adair's Action-Centered Leadership Model

of the task, and developing a high-performing team characterized by high levels of individual motivation and intragroup support.

Adair's model marked a departure from U.S. work on leadership at the time (see Stogdill, 1974) by focusing on the actions and behaviors of leaders rather than the traits or qualities of leaders. He also identified three key dimensions of leadership (represented by the three circles) rather than the two that had been the focus of much U.S. research (task-related and relationship-related behavior).

Adair's scholarship made a valuable contribution to leadership ideas and practice in many sectors and countries. This was formally recognized by the companies Hewitt and Honda in September 2005 with an award for a lifetime's contribution to leadership studies. Adair examined leadership through different lenses, focusing on the contribution of great leaders (Adair, 1989); applying his model of functional leadership to different organizational levels, from team to strategic levels (Adair, 1983, 2004); and demonstrating how leadership could be developed through training, experience, and reflection (Adair 1988, 2005). A further contribution was to break down the concept of the leadership role into a constellation of skills and behaviors that together, echoing McGregor (1960), made up "the human side of enterprise." Adair's constellation included decision making, team building, motivation, communication, creativity and innovation, and time management. These themes are now common in many leadership textbooks (Hughes, Ginnett, and Curphy, 1999).

Adair's work reached higher education through his appointment at the University of Surrey as a full professor for five years (1978–1983) and visiting professor for a further five (1984–1989). At Surrey he initiated leadership courses for students and young graduate professionals and leadership courses for heads of academic departments and other senior staff. The courses and developments for students are not the focus of this chapter, although they are significant in themselves and spawned a range of developments in engineering and other professions. The focus here is on the programs for staff and related research on leadership and management in academic organizations that helped ultimately to support the impetus behind the Leadership Foundation.

New Directions for Higher Education • DOI: 10.1002/he

Adair saw a close connection between programs for staff and students. In his inaugural professorial lecture, he identified five aspects of a systematic approach to leadership development that he believed universities should foster (Adair, 1988):

1. A short leadership studies course to raise awareness of key concepts and skills.
2. Field leadership training (such as structured work experience).
3. Staff training for academics and professionals involved in leadership development.
4. Research and development involving a partnership between academic and practitioner contributions to leadership.
5. Structure and ethos, or the ways in which a university can further good leadership. This includes project and teamwork, training and preparation for those with leadership responsibilities at all levels, nurturing the academic leadership role involved in teaching and research, the role of the university in exploring and discovering values for life and work, and the university's contribution to developing the leaders of tomorrow.

These themes are echoed in much of the work of the Leadership Foundation.

Adair's first initiative for academic staff was a two-day residential course for academic heads of department from across the United Kingdom. The content reflected his leadership constellation, and the pedagogy was inspired by Adair's belief in experiential and participative learning. Soon afterward, a new seminar for trios of more senior institutional leaders was mounted. Two years later, both courses had proved successful enough to warrant an application to the U.K. Department of Education and Science (DES) to fund further development of the programs linked to an evaluation. The final evaluation report noted that "the national programme for Heads of academic departments made a valuable contribution in the start-up phase of leadership and management training for Heads. In 1984 it was the only course of its kind; by 1988, 75 percent of universities were reportedly planning or already providing local or regional programmes, many of them incorporating aspects of the 'Action-Centred Leadership' model" (Middlehurst, 1989, p. 180).

Moving the Agenda Forward: Research, Politics and Timing

Adair's early work with universities contributed to a changing attitude toward the exercise of leadership in academic organizations and the university's role in developing its own leaders. The vice chancellor of the University of London at the time, Lord Flowers, captured the beginnings of this spirit of change, commenting: "We have to look to our leaders of the future . . . [to create] . . . a climate in which leadership can flourish rather than be restrained by precedent and the safety belt of committee decisions" (quoted in Adair, 1988, p. 128). Change was pushed further in the following year through the national Jarratt Report, which investigated the efficiency of management and decision making in universities. The authors recommended changes in the structure and governance of institutions to strengthen the power of executive management (Committee of Vice Chancellors and Principals, 1985). Similar analyses and recommendations were occurring in the United States at this time with calls for better and more visionary leadership in higher education (see, for example, "To Reclaim a Legacy," Bennett, 1984). The American Council on Education also argued the case for stronger leadership and management in universities (Green, 1988). However, other scholars were more skeptical about what was known as the leadership crisis in American higher education and the faith shown in the power and wisdom of leadership to make a difference to institutional performance (Bensimon, Neumann, and Birnbaum, 1989).

In the United Kingdom, the DES-funded evaluation and development project provided an opportunity to examine the views of academic heads of department about their growing leadership and management responsibilities. In all, 175 participants were surveyed, with an 81 percent response rate. Course evaluation forms were also assessed, and interviews with a smaller sample of heads (thirty-three interviews in fourteen institutions) were undertaken. This research also offered an opportunity to explore perspectives on the context of declining state funding and increasing student enrollments that accompanied the changing expectations of the role of heads of department (Middlehurst, 1989; Middlehurst, Pope, and Wray, 1991).

A second project (1989–1991), building on the first one, investigated the changing expectations of the roles of more senior staff, examining perceptions of leadership and management and leadership development needs at different levels of an institution. Ten universities were included in this study (out of a total population at the time in the United Kingdom of some fifty universities). There were 251 people interviewed, and an 86 percent response rate was achieved from a questionnaire survey of fifty senior staff. In parallel in the United States, a more detailed and extensive five-year longitudinal study of institutional leadership (the Institutional Leadership Project) facilitated comparisons between the U.K. and U.S. contexts and the range of views concerning higher education leadership and management. These three studies from the United Kingdom and the United States provided valuable data for the development and subsequent work of the Leadership Foundation.

The evaluation of the Adair leadership courses brought into sharp relief the contrasting attitudes of academic heads of department to the application of management and leadership concepts to universities (particularly concepts drawn from industrial, military, and commercial settings). Respondents drew attention to the distinctiveness of universities as organizations as well as to the receptiveness or otherwise of their institutions toward more executive styles of management. The question of differences between management and leadership was also raised. Comments highlighted:

- The difficulties of managing change in universities where strong democratic and antimanagerial traditions existed
- The problem of managing highly individualistic academics with no strong sense of corporate identity to department or university
- Insufficient departmental autonomy to carry management through
- Lack of a management ethos in the faculty and resistance to one in the university as a whole
- Difficulties of implementing leadership on account of vagueness of institutional objectives, endless talking, and few decisions, further hindered by recent financial cuts
- The need for a level of understanding of management concepts and the freedom to exercise degrees of control and influence in order to exercise effective leadership

For some participants, university culture and ethos made the course content difficult to apply in practice or not relevant conceptually. For others, the courses helped to create a positive approach to effective departmental management and new conceptions of the parameters of the job. These divided and contrasting views about the applicability of leadership and management concepts to universities (and Adair's model in particular) were an intriguing product of this study. Such views have been highlighted in more recent research in Australia and the United Kingdom (Ramsden, 1998; Deem, 1998).

The second DES-funded study (Middlehurst, Pope, and Wray, 1991) focused more deeply on the changing operating environment, highlighting increasing levels of public scrutiny of universities and the associated management and developmental responses. Such public scrutiny is now widespread in higher education reforms around the world that focus on efficiency and accountability in the use of public funds, value for money in the deployment of resources, combined with pressure to increase entrepreneurial activities and enhance the quality of individual and institutional performance. The U.K. study, which considered the impact of change on institutional cultures and structures, individual and collective roles, and associated skills and experience, should resonate with experiences of higher education reform in other countries.

The research noted changes in the management roles of senior staff, a redefining of management structures and processes, and an increasing burden of strategic management and leadership. University management was being strengthened through extending management and leadership responsibilities and roles across different levels of the institution. As a practical response, respondents saw a need for more targeted and systematic training and development in order to respond to new or changing roles and expectations

(Middlehurst, Pope, and Wray, 1991). This is not to say that such changes were uncontested or that training was seen as necessary or desirable by all respondents. Indeed, some responses to the notion of leadership and management training for academics were strong enough to suggest a clash of cultures; they appeared to offend underlying belief systems or cults of academic life (Middlehurst, 1993), for example:

• The cult of the gifted amateur (any intelligent, well-educated individual can undertake a leadership role without training)
• The cult of heredity (those with natural talent will rise to leadership without training)
• The cult of deficiency (training is essentially remedial and only those who prove to be ineffective need it)
• The cult of inadequacy (once a person is elevated to a role or position, loss of face results from admitting gaps in knowledge or competence)
• The cult of the implicit (learning should take place through gradual induction to the norms and expectations of academic life rather than through more explicit and formal routes)
• The cult of selection (selecting good staff will obviate the need for, and cost of, development)
• The cult of the intellectual (there is no scientific basis to management, particularly university management, so the practice of management does not warrant focused attention through training or development)

The evidence and analysis provided by the two U.K. studies, the example and wider takeup of the Adair-inspired leadership programs, and the pressures of a changing economic and political operating environment prompted a first national response by university leaders. In 1991, the Committee of Vice Chancellors and Principals (CVCP) established a central unit to promote and support staff development for all categories of staff (the Universities Staff Development Unit). This was an important initiative, but for some years, the specific focus on leadership and management, particularly at the level of senior staff, was diminished. This changed in 1999 with the launch of the Top Management Programme for Higher Education, led by two of Adair's former colleagues. The design of this nine-month program was influenced by a range of models, including the American Council of Education's Fellows Program in the United States, the European seminar for new rectors of universities, and the U.K. government's Top Management Programme.

Despite the launch of the Top Management Programme, there remained a concern that the United Kingdom was giving inadequate attention at the national and institutional levels to the training and support of individuals for the increasingly significant and complex tasks of leading, managing, and governing universities and colleges. The Higher Education Funding Council for England launched a funding initiative to support the development of effective management practice, voting £10 million over a three-year period to support developmental projects. A successful bid to this fund provided a further opportunity for research. A survey of the character, purpose, and volume of management development provision for senior managers in U.K. higher education was undertaken alongside a comparison of provision in a sample of public sectors in the United Kingdom and higher education overseas (Middlehurst and Garrett, 2001). The findings categorized institutional approaches along a continuum from nonformal and individualized (about two-thirds of the sector), to more formalized and integrated approaches to leadership and management development within an institutionwide framework linked to institutional objectives. A small number of institutions (some 2 to 5 percent) offered a structured but flexible mix of institutionally and individually targeted development. A set of case studies showcased some of the most innovative approaches.

The comparative data also highlighted weaknesses in higher education. The other public sectors surveyed had invested more in leadership and management development within a structured framework, while countries such as the United States also appeared to be ahead of the United Kingdom in terms of tailored provision, support for innovation and development, and an overall strategy for leadership and management development. These findings were made more stark by widespread recognition of the increasingly competitive international economic and political context for both higher education and the United Kingdom in general (Council for Excellence in Management and Leadership, 2002).

The research galvanized Universities UK (formerly the Committee of Vice Chancellors and Principals) to consultations with the sector and government. A steering committee produced a business case and business plan for a new national organization with a central focus on leadership, management, and governance. The U.K. funding councils provided £10 million start-up funding, and the previous Staff Development unit (now called the Higher Education Staff Development Agency) was absorbed into a new Leadership Foundation for Higher Education (LFHE). It retained relevant activities such as the Top Management Programme. The vision of the new organization is focused on the dual challenge that research and earlier experience had identified: strengthen practice and change attitudes toward leadership and management and leadership development in higher education. The target is for "the leadership, governance and management of UK higher education institutions to be regarded as world-class. Excellence in leadership and management should be recognised and held in the same high esteem as excellence in research, teaching and learning" (Leadership Foundation for Higher Education, 2004, p. 1).

The Leadership Foundation in Action: Challenges and Opportunities

The Leadership Foundation can draw on a rich inheritance of comparative research, developmental activity, and networks of practice. It is using this experience to create an innovative (and perhaps unique at this time) approach. This section of the chapter illustrates this approach in terms of organizational design and funding, a thematic and integrated focus, a range of developmental initiatives and opportunities, and positioning as champion and challenger.

Organizational Design and Funding. The foundation has a small core of staff with developmental and service functions. Staff are drawn from higher education and the wider public and private sectors, with contracts ranging from permanent to short term and secondments (fixed terms). The headquarters location is London, but staff are also located in Scotland and the north of England, with a spread of regional responsibilities across the United Kingdom. The team of seventeen staff and a wider range of associates, recruited through open advertisement and selection, is responsible for the delivery of programs and projects. Members of the governing board were recruited through advertisement and are drawn from all sectors. The chair is from the private sector, and the chief executive is also drawn from outside higher education. Constitutionally, the foundation is a charity and company limited by guarantee, thus giving it a degree of independence.

Seed funding (over three years) was provided from government sources through the funding councils. However, the foundation aims to achieve longer-term sustainability through institutional subscriptions and sales of products and services. Membership of the LFHE in 2004–2005 totaled 162 higher education institutions and related agencies, including a growing international membership.

Thematic and Integrated Focus. The foundation combines four integrated work streams: developing individuals, building institutional capacity in leadership, governance and management, and creating learning networks and generating ideas and innovation. In addition, there are three cross-cutting themes to LFHE's work: focusing on diversity, drawing on practice in other sectors, and learning from international experience. The foundation uses a variety of avenues to deliver these cross-cutting themes. These include partnerships with other organizations, affirmative action in relation to program participation, playing a leading role in cross-sector networks, joint advertising and Web linking of programs and activities, recruitment of staff with diverse expertise and experience, and cofunding of projects with relevant organizations. Cross-sector membership of the board is also invaluable.

To guide its international strategy, the LFHE has established an international reference network with high-level institutional and agency members drawn from many parts of the world (for example, the World Bank, UNESCO, and the Organization for Economic Cooperation and Development). In early 2006, drawing on this international membership, the LFHE mounted an international leadership summit to discuss the global leadership role of universities, the role of institutional leadership in internationalizing the university, and the contribution of leadership development to these agendas. Specific partnerships with parallel organizations such as the

American Council on Education, the European University Association, and the global Center for Creative Leadership facilitate study exchanges, joint development of programs for senior leaders and managers, and access to up-to-date knowledge of leadership development initiatives and innovation (Center for Creative Leadership, 2004).

The LFHE offers both a present orientation toward the strengthening of existing practice and a future orientation. The latter is represented in programs (for example, through scenario planning events) and a cross-organizational research post. This post is colocated with the Observatory on Borderless Higher Education (OBHE), a global strategic information service for higher education set up in 2002 by Universities UK and the Association of Commonwealth Universities. The OBHE's audience of national bodies and ministries, international agencies, and senior managers and leaders in higher education is similar to the LFHE's target audience. By combining and leveraging resources, the foundation gains access to a wider range of knowledge-based products for its own clients, and the observatory increases the range and depth of its coverage on leadership, governance, and management issues and their developmental implications and outcomes.

Range of Developmental Initiatives and Opportunities. The four work streams and cross-cutting themes provide opportunities for piloting and delivering a variety of developmental interventions and learning opportunities for the sector. Indicative examples are given for each work stream in Table 4.1.

The foundation recognizes the diversity and autonomy of the higher education sector in the United Kingdom, as well as the diversity of individuals, professions, and communities. Not only is its range of activities diverse, the learning processes deployed are varied, including the use of diagnostic assessments (such as 360-degree review processes), live case studies and visits, international twinning projects, case studies, institution-based projects, action learning, mentoring, coaching, research, and the use of stories and theater. There is also a deeper reason for the variety offered. The intention is also to challenge traditional approaches and conceptions of leadership and management development in the higher education sector in order to increase levels of engagement, demonstrate the personal and professional benefit of such development, and highlight (and test) different pedagogical approaches.

Role and Positioning: Champion and Challenge. The business case for the foundation rested on a set of linked rationales:

• A more competitive and challenging external environment for institutions required stronger investment in the selection, training, and support of leaders and managers.
• There was insufficient investment and engagement in the development of leadership, governance, and management in higher education.

Table 4.1. Examples of the Leadership Foundation's Activities

Work Stream	Activity	Characteristics
Supporting and developing individuals	Development center Leadership programs for managers and leaders Governor development National mentoring scheme International exchanges and visits	Systematic self-assessment for individuals Top management, senior strategic leaders, preparing for strategic,and research leadership New and experienced governors; dialogues between the vice chancellor and chair Brokers and supports mentoring arrangements Transnational leadership development
Building institutional capacity	Strategic collaboration Tailored consultancy Change Academy LFHE fellowships Succession planning Regional or national needs analysis	Focus on leading partnerships Top team support, change management, coaching Program for institutional teams with change agendas Fund for institutional change projects Background research on current practice and cross-sector comparisons Nationwide institutional and stakeholder consultation and survey pioneered in Scotland
Creating learning networks	Human resources, finance, estates, library and information services, deputy vice chancellors, heads of administration	Codesign of specialist programs and activities
Generating ideas and innovation	Commissioned program of research on higher education leadership, governance, and management Small development projects Knowledge-based resources	Gender and leadership, changing senior roles and development implications, leadership of teaching, strategic collaboration, distributed leadership, leadership and effectiveness in higher education Practice-based project funding Purchase of licenses for Web-based resources on behalf of members

• The practice of leadership, governance, and management was not always held in high esteem within the sector or by some stakeholders from the lay community and government. Sources of evidence for this point differed. Within the sector, some institutions reported increasing difficulty in attracting academics to key management positions (such as heads of department or deans). Externally, higher education management was not infrequently compared unfavorably with private sector practice by politicians and the media (despite countervailing evidence such as provided by the findings of the Lambert report, 2003, on university-business collaboration in the United Kingdom).

The task of the foundation was therefore conceived as delivering a substantive development agenda and providing a challenge to internal and external perceptions of higher education management and leadership. Achieving cultural change of this kind is a long-term game involving a range of symbolic and substantive mechanisms. The foundation's marketing and communications strategy is as important here as the development of an evidence base of research. The communications strategy includes printed newsletters, briefing papers, and reports, as well as Web-based and electronic materials. Media coverage and political engagement are also key focuses. The foundation's independent position within the sector facilitates high-level roundtable discussions (observing the Chatham House Rule of political topics, which facilitates free speech while protecting confidentiality at meetings, so participants feel freer to contribute to an honest discussion of the issues), such as changing governance structures or performance management in higher education. The LFHE can act as both a champion and challenger of current practice and political perspectives of the sector.

Conclusion

The Leadership Foundation for Higher Education is a new venture in the United Kingdom built on an evidence base of research, experience, and practice drawn from the sector itself and cross-sector and international comparisons. Its agenda is ambitious, and only time will tell whether its vision will prevail. Two years from its establishment, the foundation has just undergone an independent evaluation initiated by its funders. This strongly positive evaluation will assist the foundation in its future development and its continuing role in support of excellence in higher education leadership, governance, and management.

References

Adair, J. *Training for Leadership.* Aldershot: Gower, 1968.
Adair, J. *Effective Leadership.* London: Pan, 1983.
Adair, J. *Developing Leaders.* Guildford: Talbot Adair Press, 1988.

Adair, J. *Great Leaders.* Guildford: Talbot Adair Press, 1989.
Adair, J. *Effective Strategic Leadership.* London: Kogan Page, 2004.
Adair, J. *How to Grow Leaders.* London: Kogan Page, 2005.
Bennett, W. *To Reclaim a Legacy: A Report on the Humanities in Higher Education.* Washington, D.C.: National Endowment for the Humanities, 1984.
Bensimon, E., Neumann, A., and Birnbaum, R. *Making Sense of Administrative Leadership: The "L" Word in Higher Education.* Washington, D.C.: ASHE-ERIC, 1989.
Center for Creative Leadership. *Handbook of Leadership Development.* (2nd ed.) San Francisco: Jossey-Bass, 2004.
Committee of Vice Chancellors and Principals. *Report of the Steering Committee on Efficiency Studies in Universities.* London: Committee of Vice Chancellors and Principals, 1985.
Council for Excellence in Management and Leadership. *Managers and Leaders: Raising Our Game: Final Report.* London: Council for Excellence in Management and Leadership, 2002.
Deem, R. "'New Managerialism' and Higher Education: The Management of Performance and Cultures in Universities in the United Kingdom." *International Studies in Higher Education,* 1998, 8(1), 47–70.
Fayol, H. *General Industrial Management.* London: Pitman, 1949.
Green, M. *Leaders for a New Era: Strategies for Higher Education.* New York: ACE/Macmillan, 1988.
Green, M., and McDade, S. *Investing in Higher Education: A Handbook of Leadership Development.* New York: ACE/Macmillan, 1991.
Hughes, R., Ginnett, R., and Curphy, G. *Leadership: Enhancing the Lessons of Experience.* New York: McGraw-Hill, 1999.
Lambert, R. *Lambert Review of Business-University Collaboration: Final Report.* London: Her Majesty's Stationery Office, 2003.
Leadership Foundation for Higher Education. *Prospectus.* London: Leadership Foundation for Higher Education, 2004.
Lewin, K. "Dynamics of Group Action." *Educational Leadership,* 1944, 1, 195–200.
Maslow, A. *Motivation and Personality.* New York: HarperCollins, 1954.
Matheson, C. *Staff Development Matters: Academic Staff Training and Development in Universities of the United Kingdom.* London: Central Committee for the Training of University Teachers, 1981.
McGregor, D. *The Human Side of Enterprise.* New York: McGraw-Hill, 1960.
Middlehurst, R. *Leadership Development in Universities, 1986–1988: Final Report to the Department of Education and Science.* Surrey: University of Surrey, 1989.
Middlehurst, R. *Leading Academics.* Buckingham: SRHE/Open University Press, 1993.
Middlehurst, R., and Garrett, R. *Developing Senior Managers.* Summary Report and Vol. 2: *Supporting Evidence.* (HESDA Archive: http://www.lfhe.ac.uk/Hesda), 2001.
Middlehurst, R., Pope, M., and Wray, M. *The Changing Roles of University Managers and Leaders: Implications for Preparation and Development: Final Report to the Department for Education and Science.* Surrey: University of Surrey, 1991.
Ramsden, P. *Learning to Lead in Higher Education.* London: Routledge, 1998.
Stogdill, R. *Handbook of Leadership.* New York: Free Press, 1974.
World Bank. *Constructing Knowledge Societies: New Challenges for Tertiary Education.* Washington, D.C.: World Bank, 2002.

ROBIN MIDDLEHURST *is professor of higher education at the University of Surrey and director of the university's Centre for Policy and Change in Tertiary Education.*

5

The Baldrige quality criteria generate a number of questions that can make accreditation self-studies more productive.

Higher Education Assessment: Linking Accreditation Standards and the Malcolm Baldrige Criteria

Brent D. Ruben

It is difficult to overstate the importance of the societal role played by higher education. Colleges and universities contribute immeasurably to the personal and professional lives of students and enrich the intellectual, economic, and cultural fabric of their communities, states, nations, and beyond. As Frank Rhodes, president emeritus of Cornell put it, higher education

> . . . informs public understanding, cultivates public taste, and contributes to the nation's well-being as it nurtures and trains each new generation of architects, artists, authors, business leaders, engineers, farmers, lawyers, physicians, poets, scientists, social workers, and teachers as well as a steady succession of advocates, dreamers, doers, dropouts, parents, politicians, preachers, prophets, social reformers, visionaries, and volunteers who leaven, nudge, and shape the course of public life [Rhodes, 2001, p. xi].

Our colleges and universities have ensured that U.S. higher education is "at the forefront of our society as gatekeepers for the knowledge, creativity, and invention that can guarantee economic security and advancement" (Lawrence, 2006, p. 2).

I am grateful to Louise Sandmeyer, Christine Cermak, Phil Furmanski, Yana Grushina, and Susan Jurow for thoughts that contributed to this chapter; however, the responsibility for the integration and presentation of these ideas rests solely with me.

Few other social institutions have been as treasured as colleges and universities. Indeed, the individual and societal benefits of higher education have been broadly recognized for so long that many within the academic community have come to take this state of affairs for granted. Unfortunately, the pattern of unconditional positive regard has been changing. Particularly in the past two decades, colleges and universities have come under increasing scrutiny and critique from within and outside the academy. Most often, criticism has centered on issues of value, quality, cost, accountability, access, mission appropriateness, and faculty and staff productivity (Burke and Serban, 1997; Ewell, 1994; Kellogg Commission, 1996, 2000, 2001a, 2001b; Lawrence, 2006; Massy, 2003; Ruben, 1995, 2004; Weinstein, 1993; Wilson, 2001; Wingspread Group on Higher Education, 1993). These concerns have led to calls for more vigorous review of higher education's operating practices and for a reexamination of more fundamental issues related to the purposes and aspirations of colleges and universities (Boyer Commission, 1998; Frank, 2001; Gardiner, 1994; Kellogg Commission, 1996, 2000, 2001a, 2001b; Middle States Commission, 2002; Munitz, 1995; National Association of State Universities and Land-Grant Colleges, 2001; Newman and Couturier, 2001; Ruben, 1995, 2004; Weinstein, 1993; Wingspread Group on Higher Education, 1993).

The Spellings Commission

In 2006, the deliberations of the Spellings Commission on the Future of Higher Education, initiated by Secretary of Education Margaret Spellings, brought a new level of visibility and intensity to the critique (American Council on Education, 2006; Inside Higher Ed, 2006; Spellings, 2006a, 2006b). In the preamble of the August 9 draft report, the Commission describes the current situation in this way (Spellings, 2006a, p. 3):

> Three hundred and seventy years after the first college in our fledgling nation was established . . . higher education in the United States has become one of our greatest success stories. . . . Despite these achievements, however, this Commission believes U.S. higher education needs to improve in dramatic ways. As we enter the Twenty-First Century, it is no slight to the successes of American colleges and universities thus far in our history to note the unfulfilled promise that remains. Our year-long examination of the challenges facing higher education has brought us to the uneasy conclusion that the sector's past attainments have led our nation to unwarranted complacency about its future.
>
> It is time to be frank. Among the vast and varied institutions that make up U.S. higher education, we have found much to applaud, but also much that requires urgent reform. . . . To be sure, at first glance most Americans don't see colleges and universities as a trouble spot in our educational system. . . . For a long time, we educated more people to higher levels than any other nation.

NEW DIRECTIONS FOR HIGHER EDUCATION • DOI: 10.1002/he

We remained so far ahead of our competitors for so long, however, that we began to take our postsecondary superiority for granted. The results of this inattention, though little known to many of our fellow citizens, are sobering. We may still have more than our share of the world's best universities. But a lot of other countries have followed our lead, and they are now educating more of their citizens to more advanced levels than we are. Worse, they are passing us by at a time when education is more important to our collective prosperity than ever.

To address the "urgent reform" needs identified (Spellings, 2006a), the commission offered six recommendations:

1. Every student in the nation should have the opportunity to pursue postsecondary education. We recommend, therefore, that the U.S. commit to an unprecedented effort to expand higher education access and success by improving preparation and persistence, addressing non-academic barriers and providing significant increases in aid to low-income students.
2. To address the escalating cost of a college education and the fiscal realities affecting government's ability to finance higher education in the long run, we recommend that the entire student financial aid system be restructured and new incentives put in place to improve the measurement and management of costs and institutional productivity.
3. To meet the challenges of the 21st century, higher education must change from a system primarily based on reputation to one based on performance. We urge the creation of a robust culture of accountability and transparency throughout higher education. Every one of our goals, from improving access and affordability to enhancing quality and innovation, will be more easily achieved if higher education embraces and implements serious accountability measures.
4. With too few exceptions, higher education has yet to address the fundamental issues of how academic programs and institutions must be transformed to serve the changing needs of a knowledge economy. We recommend that America's colleges and universities embrace a culture of continuous innovation and quality improvement by developing new pedagogies, curricula, and technologies to improve learning, particularly in the area of science and mathematical literacy.
5. America must ensure that our citizens have access to high quality and affordable educational, learning, and training opportunities throughout their lives. We recommend the development of a national strategy for lifelong learning that helps all citizens understand the importance of preparing for and participating in higher education throughout their lives.
6. The United States must ensure the capacity of its universities to achieve global leadership in key strategic areas such as science, engineering,

NEW DIRECTIONS FOR HIGHER EDUCATION • DOI: 10.1002/he

medicine, and other knowledge-intensive professions. We recommend increased federal investment in areas critical to our nation's global competitiveness and a renewed commitment to attract the best and brightest minds from across the nation and around the world to lead the next wave of American innovation [pp. 17–25].

Although these issues are not new, the strident language and broad distribution of the Commission's reports and communiqués, coupled with the official status of the group and concerns about increased external regulation, have prompted vigorous reactions from many quarters (Berdahl, 2006; Field, 2006; Inside Higher Ed, 2006; Lederman, 2006a, 2006b, 2006c, 2006d; McPherson, 2006; Spellings, 2006b; U.S. Department of Education, 2006; Ward, 2006).

At issue in this and earlier discussions of the future of U.S. higher education is what Donald Kennedy (1997, p. 2) describes as a "kind of dissonance between the purposes our society foresees for the university and the way the university sees itself." In *Pursuing Excellence in Higher Education: Eight Fundamental Challenges,* Ruben (2004) characterized this situation as a tension between the traditional values of the academy and the values of the contemporary marketplace.

Assessment: Center Stage in the National Dialogue on the Future of Higher Education

The work of the Spellings Commission has focused attention on a number of concepts, but none more vigorously than assessment (Miller, 2006; Schray, 2006; Spellings, 2006a); the concept, and associated notions of accountability and transparency, have been central themes in the documents and the ensuing dialogue.

The term *assessment* triggers emotions ranging from unbridled enthusiasm to acute anxiety at the prospect of more—or less—attention to outcomes measurement, fact-based evaluation of classroom learning, institutional effectiveness and efficiency, transparency and standardization of evaluative criteria and processes, measurement of value-added, external regulation, accountability, and, most basic, fundamental change in the avowed purposes of U.S. higher education.

While these are important topics for discussion, questions about underlying motives, hidden agendas, and the potential increase in national regulation are barriers to what would otherwise be useful and constructive discussions. The plethora of connotations and valences associated with the term *assessment* represent another significant impediment to meaningful dialogue. If assessment were described in neutral and generic terms, it would be difficult to find anyone inside or outside higher education who would argue with its value. Who would disagree with the assertion that it is essential to determine, document, and ensure the quality of the work within

NEW DIRECTIONS FOR HIGHER EDUCATION • DOI: 10.1002/he

colleges and universities? Indeed, this is a core value within the academy. Issues related to the review of the contributions of students, faculty, staff, programs, and institutions have always been a central concern within colleges and universities, and a substantial amount of time and energy are devoted to these activities within all institutions. Moreover, there is no shortage of reflective writings on the topic in popular, professional, and academic literature (Astin, 1993; Burke, 1997; Burke and Minassians, 2001; Burke and Serban, 1997; Ewell, 1994; Frank, 2001; Jackson and Lund, 2000; Kuh, 2001; Light, 2001; Newman and Couturier, 2001; Pascarella, 2001; Ruben, 2001a, 2004, 2005a; Selingo, 1999; Seymour, 1989; Spangehl, 2000, 2004; Terenzini and Pascarella, 1994; Wilson, 2001).

Accreditation

One of the most visible influences for reflective review within higher education is accreditation. Through a process that includes self-study and peer review, the professional, special focus, and regional accrediting agencies provide a regularized, structured mechanism for quality assurance and improvement for the U.S. higher education community (Eaton, 2005). The Council for Higher Education Accreditation (CHEA) has some eighty accrediting member organizations that oversee the review and accreditation for some seven thousand institutions and seventeen thousand programs (Council for Higher Education Accreditation, 2000; Eaton, 2005). Typically the review process takes place every three to ten years, and it consists of the following steps:

- A self-evaluation by an institution or program using the standards or criteria of an accrediting organization
- A peer review of an institution or program to gather evidence of quality
- A decision or judgment by an accrediting organization to accredit, accredit with conditions, or not accredit an institution or program (Council for Higher Education, 2000)

Notwithstanding assertions that the process could benefit from being more transparent and standardized (Schray, 2006; Spellings, 2000a, Spellings, 2000b), there is no question that the regional accrediting associations, as well as the professional and other associations, have been a driving force in promoting increasing attention to assessment, planning, and continuous improvement through their standards and guidelines (American Council on Education, 2006; Eaton, 2006; Middle States Commission on Higher Education, 2002; Middle States Commission on Higher Education, 2006; North Central Association of Colleges and Schools, 2004; Northwest Commission on Colleges and Universities, 2004; Southern Association of Colleges and Schools, 2003; Spangehl, 2000, 2004; Western Association of Schools and Colleges, 2004).

NEW DIRECTIONS FOR HIGHER EDUCATION • DOI: 10.1002/he

The description provided by the Western Association of Schools and Colleges is quite typical in this regard: one of the primary goals of accreditation is "promoting within institutions a culture of evidence where indicators of performance are regularly developed and data collected to inform institutional decision making, planning, and improvement" (2004, p. 6).

Within colleges and universities, program and, especially, institution-wide accreditation reviews are viewed as major events, often requiring several years for self-study, the preparation of substantial documentation, peer review, and follow-up. In times when resource and accountability pressures were less intense, the academic mission and programs of colleges and universities provided the primary focus for institutional accreditation. In the current environment, the broad challenges confronting higher education—national, state and institutional pressures for fiscal constraint, accountability, attention to learning outcomes assessment, productivity measurement, mission clarity and distinctiveness, and institutional structure—all converge in discussions of accreditation.

Contemporary accreditation standards and practices give far more attention to measurement and outcomes and less to intentions and inputs than in earlier periods. Underpinning this shift is an expanded focus on the received experience of students as distinct institutional intentions, structures, expertise, and plans of faculty and staff (Ruben, 2005d). More attention is also being given to assessing the effectiveness of the institution or program more holistically, as an organization. Additional effort is also devoted to evaluating student learning and the value added by the learning experience–and for residential colleges and universities, the living experience—provided by the institution. It is worth noting that the growing interest in assessment is not unique to higher education; the trend toward increasing emphasis on the measurement of performance in terms of outputs and value added has become pervasive in business, health care, and government as well (Brancato, 1995; Kaplan and Norton, 1992, 1996, 2001; Ruben, 2004).

Traditionally, the primary—and the most interested—audience for accreditation was the higher education community itself (Eaton, 2005). The process fostered programmatic and institutional self-examination and peer review, and the results were used to guide refinements within the institutions involved. With growing concerns about accountability, value, access, and quality, accreditation has come to serve an increasingly significant gatekeeper function for external constituencies, including federal and state governments and the general public (Eaton, 2005). As CHEA president Judith Eaton (2005) notes, "Accreditation [now] has many masters and mistresses." As articulated by one of the regional associations, the accreditation process "stimulates evaluation and improvement, while providing a means of continuing accountability to constituents and the public" (Southern Association of Colleges and Schools, 2003, p. 3).

As accreditation evolves to serve a broader array of stakeholders and functions, there has been an understandable concomitant shift toward increasingly systemic reviews of institutions and programs. This broadened the perspective that acknowledges the contribution of all component units and functions—academic, but also student affairs, services, and administration—to the overall success of a program or institution (Ruben, 2004). There may have been a time, for example, when the excellence of institutions or programs was assumed to be a natural and inevitable consequence of having distinguished faculty members—and hence quality review could focus primarily on individual faculty accomplishments. Today, however, there is a growing recognition that a more multifaceted and nuanced perspective is required, as it has become apparent that institutional or programmatic excellence is contingent on many factors beyond the excellence of individual faculty members (Ruben, 2004). It also seems reasonable to assume that the aggressive external critique of the accreditation process will accelerate the progression toward more comprehensive, outcome-based, and systematic reviews (Schray, 2006; Spellings, 2006a, 2006b).

The Baldrige Framework

Of the various rigorous and systemic approaches to the assessment, planning, and improvement of organizations, none has been more successful or more influential than the Malcolm Baldrige model (Baldrige, 2006a). The Malcolm Baldrige National Quality Award Program (MBNQA) was established by the U.S. Congress in 1987. Named after Secretary of Commerce Malcolm Baldrige, who served from 1981 until his death in 1987, the intent of the program is to promote U.S. business effectiveness for the advancement of the national economy by providing a systems approach for organizational assessment and improvement. More specifically, the goals of the program are to:

- Identify the essential components of organizational excellence
- Recognize organizations that demonstrate these characteristics
- Promote information sharing by exemplary organizations
- Encourage the adoption of effective organizational principles and practices

   The program, which is administered by the National Institute for Standards and Technology (NIST), has also been important in national and international efforts to identify and encourage the application of core principles of organizational excellence. The number of state, local, and regional award programs based on the Baldrige increased from eight programs in 1991 to forty-three programs in 1999 (Calhoun, 2002; Vokurka, 2001), and over twenty-five different countries have used the Baldrige criteria as the basis for their own national awards (Przasnyski and Tai, 2002). Subsequently, this number has increased to over sixty national awards in other countries (Vokurka, 2001). One notable example is the European Quality Foundation Model (European Foundation for Quality Management, 2006).

NEW DIRECTIONS FOR HIGHER EDUCATION • DOI: 10.1002/he

If the broadly stated purpose of the accreditation process is to "stimulate . . . evaluation and improvement, while providing a means of continuing accountability to constituents and the public" (Southern Association of Colleges and Schools, 2003, p. 3), this same description applies to the Malcolm Baldrige framework. As with accreditation frameworks, the Baldrige approach emphasizes the need to broadly define excellence; value leadership and planning; establish clear, shared, and measurable goals; create effective programs and departments; conduct systematic assessments of outcomes; engage in comparisons with peers and leaders; and make improvements based on the results of the assessment.[1] As with accrediting, the presupposition of the Baldrige framework is that the iterative process of review, planning, continuous improvement, and assessment is fundamental to institutional effectiveness and should be thoroughly integrated into the fabric of every institution aspiring to excellence (Baldrige, 2006a; Middle States Commission on Higher Education, 2002; North Central Association of Colleges and Schools, 2004).

The Baldrige framework consists of seven categories. Although the language and definitions used to describe the framework have changed over the years, and vary somewhat from sector to sector, the seven basic themes remain constant. In general terms, the framework suggests that organizational excellence requires:

1. Effective leadership that provides guidance and ensures a clear and shared sense of organizational mission and future vision, a commitment to continuous review and improvement of leadership practice, and social and environmental consciousness
2. An inclusive planning process and coherent plans that translate the organization's mission, vision, and values into clear, aggressive, and measurable goals that are understood and effectively implemented throughout the organization
3. Knowledge of the needs, expectations, and satisfaction and dissatisfaction levels of the groups served by the organization; programs, services, and practices that are responsive to these needs and expectations; and assessment processes in place to stay current with and anticipate the thinking of these groups
4. Development and use of indicators of organizational quality and effectiveness that capture the organization's mission, vision, values, and goals and provide data-based comparisons with peer and leading organizations; widely sharing this and other information within the organization to focus and motivate improvement
5. A workplace culture that encourages, recognizes, and rewards excellence, employee satisfaction, engagement, professional development, commitment, and pride and synchronizes individual and organizational goals
6. Focus on mission-critical and support programs and services and associated work processes to ensure effectiveness, efficiency, appropriate

standardization and documentation, and regular evaluation and improvement—with the needs and expectations of stakeholders in mind

7. Documented, sustained positive outcomes relative to organizational mission, vision, goals, the perspectives of groups served, and employees, considered in the light of comparisons with the accomplishments of peers, competitors, and leaders (Ruben, 2004)

The Baldrige model has been an extremely popular framework for organizational self-assessment. NIST estimates that thousands of organizations have used the criteria for self-assessment (Calhoun, 2002), and evidence from modeling studies supports the general theory expressed through the MBNQA criteria (Wilson and Collier, 2000). Other researchers have found that "the theory is sound . . . and [the framework] has improved since its inception" (Flynn and Saladin, 2001, p. 642).

Further evidence suggests that the Baldrige provides a valuable gauge of organizational effectiveness. A study by the Government Accountability Office of twenty companies that scored high in the Baldrige process found that these results corresponded with increased job satisfaction, improved attendance, reduced turnover, improved quality, reduced cost, increased reliability, increased on-time delivery, fewer errors, reduced lead time (customers), improved satisfaction, fewer complaints, higher customer retention rates (profitability), improved market share, and improved financial indicators (Heaphy and Gruska, 1995).

There is also further evidence that from a financial perspective, MBNQA winning organizations outperform other organizations. Przasnyski and Tai's analysis (2002) demonstrates that organizations that have been recognized as leaders by the Baldrige perform well in the marketplace and, specifically, that "companies derive the most benefit through evaluating and responding to the [Baldrige] guidelines" (p. 486). And there is evidence that these organizations excel in both growth and profits. The collected Baldrige award winners have substantially outperformed the Standard and Poor's 500 index—by about two to five times—in all but one year during the past decade (Baldrige National Quality Award, 2000). Furthermore, Rajan and Tamimi found that "companies that demonstrate their commitment to . . . Baldrige core values and concepts generate solid returns that ultimately benefit shareholders" (1999, p. 42).

In sum, there is a good deal of evidence to suggest that organizations rating highly on Baldrige standards are more successful than others, providing support for assertions that the Baldrige criteria provide a standard of excellence to which organizations can and should aspire.

Baldrige in Higher Education

One of the great virtues of the Baldrige framework is its flexibility. Although the general factors associated with excellence and effectiveness are quite

NEW DIRECTIONS FOR HIGHER EDUCATION • DOI: 10.1002/he

common across a broad array of organizations, there are important differences in the culture, language, and operating practices from sector to sector. Therefore, the basic Baldrige model has been adopted—but also adapted—for assessment in any number of differing organizational settings. The original application of the model was primarily in business. In 1999, the National Baldrige program released versions of the framework tailored to health care and education, and in 2006 a public sector version became available. The education criteria (Baldrige, 2006b) were intended to be generally applicable to schools and educational settings of all types and at all levels. Given this scope, the framework was designed to be broad enough to be appropriate for K–12 school systems, colleges and universities, and corporate educational providers.

Since its introduction, ninety-nine applications have been submitted from higher education departments or institutions to the national program.[2] Three applicants have been selected as winners of the award: the University of Wisconsin-Stout in 2001 (Furst-Bowe and Wentz, 2006), the University of Northern Colorado's Monfort School of Business in 2004, and Richland College in Dallas in 2005. There have been a number of college and university applications to state programs that parallel the Baldrige and several winners, including the University of Missouri-Rolla in 1995 and Iowa State University in 2004.

Beyond higher education institutions' direct participation in the formal national and state awards program, the influence of the framework in higher education has been most apparent in the evolution of accrediting standards of professional and technical education and more recently in regional accreditation. In business, engineering, health care, and education, the standards for accreditation of college and university programs have come to mirror the Baldrige framework in many respects. The regional accrediting associations, perhaps most notably the North Central Association of Schools and Colleges, the Middle States Association of Schools and Colleges, and the Southern Association of Schools and Colleges, emphasize issues that are central to the Baldrige framework such as leadership, strategic planning, assessment, and continuous improvement.[3]

The Excellence in Higher Education Framework

To further contextualize the Baldrige framework, the Excellence in Higher Education (EHE) model, designed specifically for use within colleges and universities, was developed at Rutgers University in 1994.[4] Motivating this work was the realization that it is difficult to comprehensively address the needs of all types of higher education institutions using criteria developed to be broadly applicable to all types of educational institutions at all levels. Moreover, the assessment, planning, and improvement language that is most familiar and useful for K–12 schools is quite different from that which fits best with the needs and culture of colleges and universities. The need for a higher education version of Baldrige was particularly clear in the case of large colleges and universities with multiple mission elements and a broad range of constituencies. Thus, the EHE framework was developed to adapt the basic Baldrige model to the culture, language, and mission of higher education institutions.

EHE was designed to be adaptable to the needs of a broad range of higher education institutions. It was also structured to be useful for assessment and planning activities by individual departments of all kinds within colleges and universities: business, student service, and service, as well as academic (Ruben, 2006a). The framework is appropriate for departments with academic or cocurricular programs and services that primarily benefit students and is equally applicable for considering the effectiveness of the institution—or constituent departments—in areas of research, public service and outreach, and internal support functions involving other audiences, including faculty and staff, professional and disciplinary communities, alumni, state and local government, or the general public.

The latest versions of Excellence in Higher Education (Ruben, forthcoming a, forthcoming b, forthcoming c) have expanded the earlier model to provide an integrated approach to assessment, planning, and improvement that draws on the framework of the Malcolm Baldrige Program and also on standards and language developed by U.S. college and university accrediting associations.[5] Together the Baldrige criteria and those developed by the regional accreditation organizations offer the best available standards of excellence for higher education, and it is the goal of EHE to provide a synthesis of the perspectives and language of those robust frameworks.

The EHE framework consists of seven categories or themes that are viewed as relevant to the effectiveness of any educational organization—program, department, school, college, or university. The categories are seen as components of an interrelated system, as shown in Figure 5.1.

Category 1: Leadership. Category 1 considers leadership approaches and governance systems used to guide the institution, department, or program; how leaders and leadership practices encourage excellence, innovation, and attention to the needs of individuals, groups, and/or organizations that benefit from the programs and services of the institution, department, or program; and how leadership practices are reviewed and improved.

Category 2: Strategic Planning. The strategic planning category considers how the mission, vision, and values of the institution, school, department, or program are developed and communicated; how they are translated into goals and plans; and how faculty and staff are engaged in those activities. Also considered are the ways in which goals and plans are translated into action and coordinated throughout the organization.

Figure 5.1. Excellence in Higher Education Framework

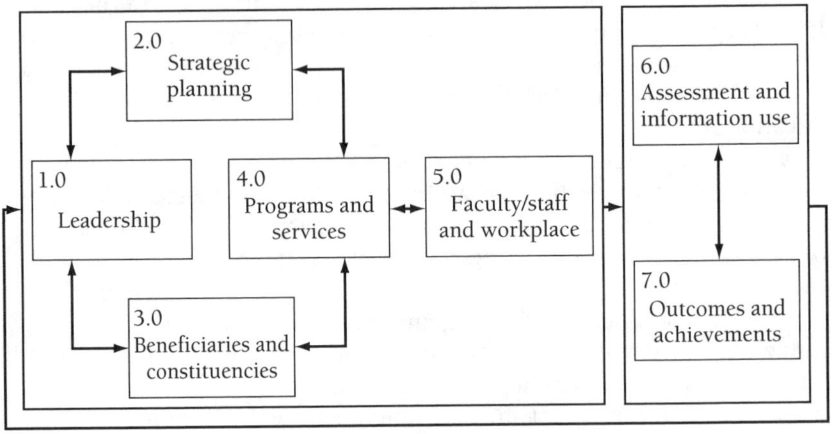

Source: Copyright 2005 by the National Association of College and University Business Officers (NACUBO). All rights reserved.

Category 3: Beneficiaries and Constituencies. The beneficiaries and constituencies category focuses on the groups that benefit from the programs and services offered by the program, department, or institution being reviewed. The category asks how the organization learns about the needs, perceptions, and priorities of those groups and how that information is used to enhance the organization's effectiveness in addressing the needs and expectations of these groups, and in building strong relationships with those constituencies.

Category 4: Programs and Services. Category 4 focuses on the programs and services offered by the institution, department, or program under review and how their quality and effectiveness are assured. The most important operational and support services are also reviewed.

Category 5: Faculty/Staff and Workplace. Category 5 considers how the program, department, or institution being reviewed recruits and retains faculty and staff; encourages excellence and engagement; creates and maintains a positive workplace culture and climate; and promotes and facilitates personal and professional development.

Category 6: Assessment and Information Use. This category focuses on how the program, department, or institution assesses its efforts to fulfill its mission and aspirations and the effectiveness of its programs and services. Also considered is how assessment information is used for improving programs and services, day-to-day decision making, and the quality of the program, department, or institution, more generally.

Category 7: Outcomes and Achievements. The category asks for information and evidence to document or demonstrate the quality and effectiveness of the program, department, or institution.

Using the EHE Framework

By intention, the EHE framework is conceptual in nature and its use is open to interpretation.

Conceptual Framework for Leaders. EHE has been used in various ways. Most basic, it can be used by leaders as a guide for conceptualizing organizational excellence at the programmatic, departmental, or institutional level and identifying specific issues that are particularly important for their effectiveness (Ruben, 2006). The *Excellence in Higher Education Guide* (Ruben, in press a) provides a set of questions to direct this thought process. In this respect, EHE has the benefit of being grounded in the substantial experience of many organizations across sectors rather than being wholly idiosyncratic or based solely on the culture or practices at a single institution.

Because EHE incorporates fundamental, broadly based, and enduring dimensions of organizational quality and effectiveness, the framework has a transferability and portability that usefully transcends particular administrations, organizations, and time frames. To the extent that the model is disseminated and widely understood and used within the department or institution, future leaders can carry the model forward conceptually and operationally rather than feeling the need to invent their own approach.

As a Guide to Organizational Assessment, Planning, and Improvement. Another common use of the EHE framework is as the basis for actively engaging the faculty or staff of a unit in assessment, planning, and improvement activities. The *EHE Guide* (Ruben, in press a), along with the companion *Workbook and Scoring Manual* (Ruben, in press b) and *Facilitator's Guide* (Ruben, in press c), are designed to support these various applications. When applied in this context, EHE can be used as the basis for a workshop or retreat that typically lasts one and one-half days. As it has been most often used, EHE workshops consist of a step-by-step assessment process, moving through the seven categories one at a time. For each category, the process includes (Ruben, in press b):

- Discussing the basic themes and standards for the category
- Brainstorming a list of strengths and areas for improvement for the unit with respect to the category
- Reviewing best practices in the category as practiced by leading organizations
- Scoring the unit in the category on a 0 to 100 percent scale to capture perceptions of the extent to which the unit is fulfilling the standards of the category[6]

The scoring for each category is conducted anonymously, the ratings are displayed, and the distribution of scores is discussed. The mean rating for the group is then calculated and entered on a chart, which is displayed

Figure 5.2. Sample Rating Chart

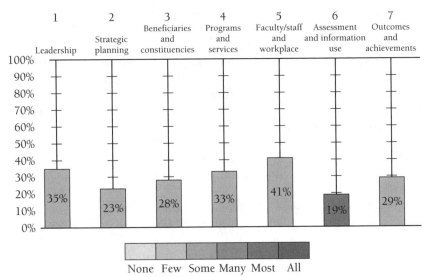

and discussed after each category and again at the conclusion of all categories. Figure 5.2 provides an example of ratings for a hypothetical department.

Once these steps have been taken for all seven categories, the list of areas of strength and those in need of improvement are reviewed and discussed further. Multivoting is then employed to rank-order the priority areas for improvement, taking account of the dimensions of importance, potential impact, and feasibility. Improvement goals and strategies are established for the highest-priority areas—generally the four to six areas perceived to be most pressing. Finally, participants in breakout groups develop preliminary plans for addressing each of the priority improvements. The preliminary plan includes a sentence summary of what needs to be done, a list of key steps, identification of the individuals or roles that should be involved in the project, a proposed team leader, a project time line, estimate of resources, and identification of important outcomes (Ruben, 2005a, 2005b). Following the workshop, it becomes the responsibility of the program, department, or institution to move forward on the improvement initiatives, periodically reporting progress to colleagues. As the selected priority projects are completed, the group could return to the list of other areas for improvement to select the next round of improvements. It is recommended that the process, illustrated in Figure 5.3, be undertaken on an annual or semiannual basis.

At Rutgers and approximately thirty other higher education institutions,[7] the EHE model has been used as an organizational self-assessment program within academic, student life, administrative, and service departments with the aim of deriving the benefits described. To date, approximately thirty-five

Figure 5.3. EHE Process

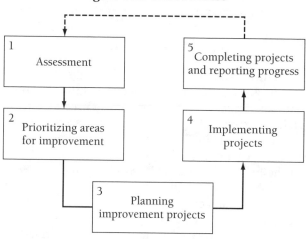

academic and administrative departments at Rutgers have participated in the program.

Value and Impact of the EHE Program. With any assessment program—accreditation, Baldrige, or EHE process—there is always the important question of whether the initiative has the desired value or impact. Within a higher education environment particularly, presumptions about and enthusiasm for any program's effectiveness are not persuasive arguments on their own.

Research on this value of Baldrige and EHE within higher education is limited. One study by Belohlav, Cook, and Heiser (2004) determined that the Baldrige framework and core values provide a useful foundation for educational planning and implementation. To study the topic further, the Center for Organizational Development and Leadership at Rutgers University has undertaken a program of research to study the value of the Baldrige program and, more specifically, the impact of the EHE approach (Ruben, 2005a).

Studies by Ruben, Connaughton, Immordino, and Lopez (2004) and Ruben, Russ, Smulowitz, and Connaughton (2006) will be briefly summarized here. The first study consisted of a Web-based survey of participants' perceptions of the EHE assessment process several months after completion of the workshops. The participating departments in this study were broadly representative of the university: three business/service/administrative departments (which provide support and programming to external university constituents, and various operational and maintenance support services to the campus community) and three units whose missions are primarily academic.

The goal of the first study was to evaluate the extent of learning, specifically participants' perceptions of the value and knowledge derived from workshop participation. The second study involved in-person interviews with department leaders approximately one year after the workshops. The research focused on organizational change by documenting improvements that have taken place in response to goals established during the earlier assessment and planning workshops.

Findings from the first study (Ruben, Connaughton, Immordino, and Lopez (2004) indicate that the EHE organizational self-assessment process does result in the acquisition of a knowledge and theory base; it also leads to the identification of strengths and improvement needs. Participants reported that as a result of the workshop, they have increased their knowledge and awareness of the Baldrige/EHE criteria and better understand the importance of the EHE categories for organizational effectiveness. Our findings also indicate that the EHE self-assessment workshop and process help participants gain a sense of where their unit stands—its strengths and areas in need of improvement—and encourages the translation of theoretical knowledge into practical improvement strategies and actions.

In discussing the perceived benefits of the Baldrige/EHE program, participants highlighted the following elements of the EHE as being the most beneficial: open discussion, consideration of performance measures, clarifying the value of planning, review of benchmarking techniques, and providing feedback on leadership effectiveness in addition to reaffirming some of the perspectives expressed in their responses to previous questions. The majority of respondents indicated that no changes were needed in the process. Roughly two-thirds of the respondents indicated that the program should be repeated every year or every other year.

The second study (Ruben, Russ, Smulowitz, and Connaughton, 2006) focused on organizational change: Did departments make substantial progress on priorities they established during the Baldrige/EHE program? Overall, the results suggest the answer is yes. Of the priorities established during the Baldrige/EHE self-assessment process, 65 percent were executed by the departments, producing "some/considerable progress." Progress ratings reported by leaders were substantiated by "improvement steps" that were found to be reflective of a priority's perceived importance.

One of the most interesting and fundamental questions raised by these studies has to do with the relationship between learning resulting from the Baldrige/EHE assessment and subsequent progress on organizational change priorities: Is there a relationship between knowledge gained from the self-assessment process and subsequent progress made on departments' EHE priorities? Findings from this study would seem intuitively to support the view that such a relationship does exist, but the design of the studies does not provide the basis for more than speculation on this point. That said, overall responses from the individual departments reported relative to organizational change suggest that leaders perceive that such a relationship exists. Moreover, side-by-side comparisons of findings regarding perceptions of knowledge acquisition in the first study and documented improvements implemented by the organization in areas identified as priorities in the

Figure 5.4. Knowledge and Process Outcomes, All Departments

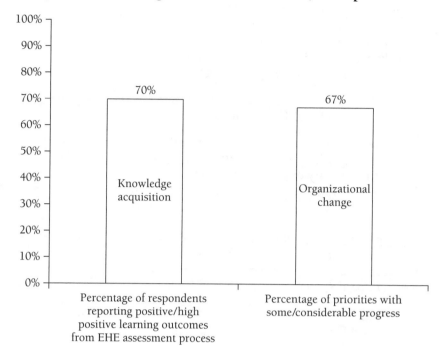

second study are also interesting. Figure 5.4 compares the knowledge acquisition and organizational change outcomes for departments that have made progress; the figures indicate the percentage of department members who evaluated the knowledge dimensions of EHE as being "valuable" or "very valuable" to their enhanced understanding and the percentage of priorities that the leaders of those departments rated as having "some" or "considerable progress." As illustrated, the knowledge outcomes (70 percent) were close to the progress on organizational change (67 percent).

To the extent that awareness and knowledge are necessary precursors to action, planning, and change, these results are most significant. They suggest that the Baldrige/EHE self-assessment process provides a solid foundation of knowledge and helps to define a standard of excellence, which contributes an important dimension to the learning process.

From our own experience and available evidence, it would seem that the EHE program can be most helpful in attaining a variety of organizational assessment, planning, and improvement goals, including these:

• Fostering organizational self-reflection
• Enhancing participant understanding of dimensions of organizational excellence
• Team building

- Increasing and enhancing communication
- Professional development
- Promoting comparisons and benchmarking
- Identifying improvement needs
- Providing a model of organizational excellence
- Performance measurement

The EHE model provides a tool for assessment that offers a number of benefits (Ruben, 2005a). This framework:

- Applies accepted standards of organizational excellence
- Is appropriate for an entire institution and for specific departments, programs, and advisory or governing groups
- Can be adapted to academic, student service, and business units
- Highlights strengths and priorities for improvement
- Creates baseline measures
- Leverages knowledge gained from other sectors
- Fosters a culture of review and improvement
- Provides a framework for sharing effective practices
- Broadens participation in leadership and problem solving
- Identifies problems and solutions that can visibly improve day-to-day operations
- Complements new and emerging accreditation models

Linking Accreditation and Baldrige

For individual programs, departments, and institutions, the evolution of accreditation presents a number of challenges but also significant opportunities. Increasingly, the process provides an opportunity to view institutional and program review less as a mandated, periodic, and compartmentalized event and more as an impetus for a proactive, empowering, and continuing campuswide planning and improvement process. The growing emphasis is on how "the institution engages in ongoing, integrated, and institution-wide research-based planning and evaluation processes that incorporate a systematic review of programs and services that (a) results in continuing improvement, and (b) demonstrates that the institution is effectively accomplishing its mission" (Southern Association of Colleges and Schools, 2003, p. 15). Thus, the challenges have to do with clarifying the mission, aspirations, and shared goals at all levels of programmatic, departmental, or institutional activity; gathering data to evaluate progress toward aspirations and goals; documenting comparisons with peer and leading programs and institutions; and systematically using the results of these analyses for improvement.[8] While most colleges and universities have long done some of this very well in some parts of the institution, few would claim that these values and practices are fully engrained in the culture.

The Baldrige/EHE framework has these same purposes. In addition, it provides a flexible conceptual framework and systematic operational tools to support integrated assessment, planning, and improvement activities at all levels of an institution. Linking accreditation with the Baldrige/EHE model leverages the strengths of two distinct yet complementary models to strengthen our approach to review and improvement in higher education.

Notes

1. For a comparative analysis of educational goals and outcomes identified by the regional and professional accrediting associations, see Association of American Colleges and Universities (2004).

2. This number, provided by the Baldrige National Quality Office in February 2006, includes some repetitive submissions.

3. See the Middle States Association of Schools and Colleges (www.msache.org), the New England Association of Schools and Colleges (www.neasc.org/cihe.htm), the North Central Association of Schools and Colleges (NCA) (www.ncahigherlearningcommission.org), the Northwest Association of Schools and Colleges (www.nwccu.org), the Southern Association of Schools and Colleges (www.sacscoc.org), and the Western Association of Schools and Colleges (www.wascweb.org). With a foundation of Baldrige concepts, the NCA has created an alternative to the accreditation model, called the Academic Quality Improvement Program, in which some two hundred institutions are currently participating.

4. The first version of this model was called Tradition of Excellence and was published in 1994 (Ruben, 1994). Revised and updated versions were published under the current name, Excellence in Higher Education, in 1994 (Ruben, 1994); 1997 (Ruben and Lehr, 1997a, 1997b); 2000 (Ruben, 2000a, 2000b, 2000c); 2001 (2001a, 2001b, 2001c), 2003 (2003a, 2003b, 2003c), and 2005 (Ruben, 2005a, 2005b, 2005c). Versions will be published in 2007 (Ruben, forthcoming a, forthcoming b, forthcoming c).

5. See the works cited in note 4.

6. In some instances, due to time restrictions or participant resistance to the idea of quantitative ratings of this type, the scoring component of the process has been omitted. Eliminating the ratings compromises the precision of the process and the possibility of clarifying the extent of similarity or difference in perceptions among participants. In other respects, it does not seem to materially alter the process or its value in other ways.

7. Higher education departments and institutions completing the Baldrige/EHE program include twelve Rutgers University business/service/administrative departments; twenty-one Rutgers University academic units; the University of California, Berkeley; University of Wisconsin, Madison; Pennsylvania State University; University of Pennsylvania; University of San Diego; California State University, Fullerton; Miami University; Raritan Valley Community College; Howard University; University at Buffalo; University of Illinois; Excelsior College; Marygrove College; Azusa Pacific University; University at Binghamton; University of Vermont; University of Massachusetts; MIT; University of Cincinnati; University of Texas, Austin; Seton Hall University; Texas A&M University; University of Toledo; and others.

8. For details on the standards for institutional accreditation, see the Council for Higher Education Accreditation (www.chea.org), the Middle States Association of Schools and Colleges (www.msache.org), the New England Association of Schools and Colleges (www.neasc.org/cihe.htm), the North Central Association of Schools and Colleges (www.ncahigherlearningcommission.org), the Northwest Association of Schools and Colleges (www.nwccu.org), the Southern Association of Schools and

Colleges (www.sacscoc.org), and the Western Association of Schools and Colleges (www.wascweb.org).

References

American Council on Education. *Addressing the Challenges Facing American Undergraduate Education.* Retrieved Sept. 21, 2006, from http://www.acenet.edu/AM/Template.cfm?Section=Home&CONTENTID=18299&TEMPLATE=/CM/ContentDisplay.cfm.

Association of American Colleges and Universities. *Taking Responsibility for the Quality of the Baccalaureate Degree.* Washington, D.C.: Association of American Colleges and Universities, 2004.

Astin, A. W. *What Matters in College?* San Francisco: Jossey-Bass, 1993.

Baldrige National Quality Award. "Baldrige: Serving Shareholders and Stakeholders." *CEO Issue Sheet,* Dec. 2000, pp. 1–2.

Baldrige National Quality Program. "Program Web Site on the National Institute of Standards and Technology Web Pages." 2006a. Retrieved Feb. 15, 2006, from www.quality.nist.gov.

Baldrige National Quality Program. *The 2006 Criteria for Performance Excellence in Education.* Washington, D.C.: National Institute of Standards and Technology, 2006b. Retrieved Feb. 15, 2006, from www.quality.nist.gov/Education_Criteria.htm.

Belohlav, J. A., Cook, L. S., and Heiser, D. R. "Using the Malcolm Baldrige National Quality Award in Teaching: One Criteria, Several Perspectives." *Decision Sciences Journal of Innovative Education,* 2004, 2(2), 153-176.

Berdahl, R. "Comments on the Second Draft of the Report of the Commission on the Future of Higher Education. American Association of Higher Education." 2006. Retrieved July 31, 2006, from http://www.aau.edu/education/AAU_Response_to_Higher _Education_Commission_Second_ Draft_Report-2006–07–31.pdf.

Boyer Commission. *Reinventing Undergraduate Education: A Blueprint for America's Research Universities.* Stony Brook: State University of New York at Stony Brook for the Carnegie Foundation, 1998.

Brancato, C. K. *New Corporate Performance Measures.* New York: Conference Board, 1995.

Burke, J. C. *Performance-Funding Indicators: Concerns, Values, and Models for Two- and Four-Year Colleges and Universities.* Albany, N.Y.: Nelson A. Rockefeller Institute of Government, 1997.

Burke, J. C., and Minassians, H. *Linking State Resources to Campus Results: From Fad to Trend—The Fifth Annual Report.* 2001. Retrieved Oct. 15, 2001, from http://www.rockinst.org/publications/higher_ed/5thSurvey.pdf.

Burke, J. C., and Serban, A. M. *Performance Funding and Budgeting for Public Higher Education: Current Status and Future Prospects.* Albany, N.Y.: Nelson A. Rockefeller Institute of Government, 1997.

Calhoun, J. M. "Using the Baldrige Criteria to Manage and Assess the Performance of Your Organization." *Journal for Quality and Participation,* 2002, 25(2), 45–53.

Council for Higher Education Accreditation. *Core Academic Values, Quality, and Regional Accreditation: The Challenge of Distance Learning.* Washington, D.C.: Council for Higher Education, 2000.

Eaton, J. S. "Accreditation and the Chief Business Officer/Chief Financial Officer." Baltimore, Md.: Annual Conference of the National Association of College and University Business Officers, 2005.

Eaton, J. S. "An Overview of U.S. Accreditation." Council of Higher Education Accreditation, 2006. Retrieved Sept. 10, 2006, from http://www.chea.org/pdf/Overview Accred_rev0706.pdf.

European Foundation for Quality Management. "European Foundation for Quality Management Model." 2006. Retrieved Feb. 10, 2006, from http://www.valuebasedmanagement.net/methods_efqm.html.

Ewell, P. "Developing Statewide Performance Indicators for Higher Education. In S. S. Ruppert (ed.), *Charting Higher Education Accountability: A Sourcebook on State-level Performance Indicators*. Denver, Colo.: Education Commission of the States, 1994.

Field, K. "Federal Panel Approves Final Draft Report on Higher Education, with One Member Dissenting." *Chronicle of Higher Education*, August 11, 2006. Retrieved Sept. 1, 2006, from http://chronicle.com/daily/2006/08/2006081101n.htm.

Flynn, B. B., and Saladin, B. "Further Evidence on the Validity of the Theoretical Model Underlying the Baldrige Criteria." *Journal of Operations Management*, 2001, *19*(6), 617–652.

Frank, R. H. "Higher Education: The Ultimate Winner-Take-All Market?" In M. E. Devlin and J. W. Meyerson (eds.), *Forum Futures: Exploring the Future of Higher Education-2000 Papers*. San Francisco: Jossey-Bass, 2001.

Furst-Bowe, J., and Wentz, M. "Beyond Baldrige: The University of Wisconsin-Stout Looks at Lessons Learned from Winning a National Quality Award." *University Business*, 2006, *9*(9), 45–48.

Gardiner, L. F. "Redesigning Higher Education." *ASHE-ERIC Higher Education Report 7*. Washington, D.C.: George Washington University, 1994.

Heaphy, M. S., and Gruska, G. F. *The Malcolm Baldrige National Quality Award: A Yardstick for Quality Growth*. Reading, Mass.: Addison-Wesley, 1995.

Inside Higher Ed. "In Focus: The Spellings Commission." *Inside Higher Ed*. Retrieved Sept. 2, 2006, from http://insidehighered.com/news/focus/commission.

Jackson, N., and Lund, H. *Benchmarking for Higher Education*. London: Society for Research into Higher Education and Open University Press, 2000.

Kaplan, R. S., and Norton, D. P. "The Balanced Scorecard—Measures That Drive Performance." *Harvard Business Review*, 1992, *70*(1), 71–79.

Kaplan, R. S., and Norton, D. P. *The Balanced Scorecard*. Boston: Harvard Business School Press, 1996.

Kaplan, R. S., and Norton, D. P. *The Strategy-Focused Organization*. Boston: Harvard Business School Press, 2001.

Kellogg Commission. *Taking Charge of Change: Renewing the Promise of State and Land-Grant Universities*. Washington, D.C.: National Association of State Universities and Land-Grant Colleges, 1996. Retrieved Mar. 10, 2002, from http://www.nasulgc.org/Kellogg/kellogg.htm.

Kellogg Commission. *Renewing the Covenant: Learning, Discovery, and Engagement in a New Age and Different World*. Washington, D.C.: National Association of State Universities and Land-Grant Colleges, 2000. Retrieved Mar. 10, 2002, from http://www.nasulgc.org/Kellogg/kellogg.htm.

Kellogg Commission. *Returning to Our Roots: Executive Summaries of the Reports of the Kellogg Commission on the Future of State and Land-Grant Universities*. Washington, D.C.: National Association of State Universities and Land-Grant Colleges, 2001a. Retrieved Mar. 10, 2002, from http://www.nasulgc.org/Kellogg/kellogg.htm.

Kellogg Commission. "Leadership for Institutional Change Initiative." 2001b. Retrieved Jan. 10, 2002, and Mar. 10, 2002, from http://www.leadershiponlinewkkf.org/.

Kennedy, D. *Academic Duty*. Cambridge, Mass.: Harvard University Press, 1997.

Kuh, G. D. "Assessing What Really Matters to Student Learning." *Change*, 2001, *33*(3), 10–17, 66.

Lawrence, F. L. *Leadership in Higher Education: Views from the Presidency*. New Brunswick, N.J.: Transaction Books, 2006.

Lederman, D. "A Stinging First Draft." *Inside Higher Ed*, June 15, 2006a. Retrieved Sept. 1, 2006, from http://insidehighered.com/news/2006/06/27/commission.

Lederman, D. "Whodunit? Chairman Miller, That's Who." *Inside Higher Ed,* Aug. 9, 2006b. Retrieved Sept. 1, 2006, from http://www.insidehighered.com/news/2006/08/09/loans.

Lederman, D. "Carrying Out the Commission's Ideas." *Insider Higher Ed,* Aug. 17, 2006c. Retrieved Sept. 1, 2006, from http://www.insidehighered.com/news/2006/08/17/commission.

Lederman, D. "Regulatory Activism." *Inside Higher Ed,* Aug. 21, 2006d. Retrieved Sept. 1, 2006, from http://insidehighered.com/news/2006/08/21/regs.

Light, R. J. *Making the Most of College: Students Speak Their Minds.* Cambridge, Mass.: Harvard University Press, 2001.

Massy, W. F. *Honoring the Trust.* Bolton, Mass.: Anker, 2003.

McPherson, P. "NASULGC President Peter McPherson Responds to the Commission on the Future of Higher Education Report. National Association of State Universities and Land-Grant Colleges." Aug. 10, 2006. Retrieved Sept. 2, 2006, from http://www.nasulgc.org/CAA/NASULGC_Commission_Response8–10.pdf.

Middle States Commission on Higher Education. *Characteristics of Excellence in Higher Education: Eligibility Requirements and Standards for Accreditation.* Philadelphia: Middle States Commission on Higher Education, 2002.

Middle States Commission on Higher Education. *Characteristics of Excellence in Higher Education: Eligibility Requirements and Standards for Accreditation.* Philadelphia: Middle States Commission on Higher Education, 2006.

Miller, C. "Issue Paper 2: Accountability/Consumer Information." Secretary of Education's Commission on the Future of Higher Education, 2006. Retrieved Sept. 1, 2006, from http://www.ed.gov/about/bdscomm/list/hiedfuture/reports/miller.pdf.

Munitz, B. "New Leadership for Higher Education." *California State University Information Bulletin,* 1995, 52(15).

National Association of State Universities and Land-Grant Colleges. *Shaping the Future: The Economic Impact of Public Universities.* Washington, D.C.: National Association of State Universities and Land-Grant Colleges, 2001.

Newman, F., and Couturier, L. K. "The New Competitive Arena: Market Forces Invade the Academy." *Change,* 2001, 33(5), 10–17.

North Central Association of Colleges and Schools, Higher Learning Commission, July 2004. *The Higher Learning Commission's Academic Quality Improvement Project.* Retrieved Aug. 1, 2004, from http://AQIP.org.

Northwest Commission on Colleges and Universities. *Accreditation Standards.* Redmond, Wash.: Northwest Commission on Colleges and Universities, 2004.

Pascarella, E. T. "Identifying Excellence in Undergraduate Education: Are We Even Close?" *Change,* 2001, 33(3), 19–23.

Przasnyski, Z., and Tai, L. S. "Stock Performance of Malcolm Baldrige National Quality Award Winning Companies." *Total Quality Management,* 2002, 13(4), 475–488.

Rajan, M., and Tamimi, N. "Baldrige Award Winners: The Payoff to Quality." *Journal of Investing,* 1999, 8(4), 39–42.

Rhodes, F. H. *The Creation of the Future: The Role of the American University.* Ithaca, N.Y.: Cornell University Press, 2001.

Ruben, B. D. *Tradition of Excellence: Higher Education Quality Self-Assessment Guide.* Dubuque, Iowa: Kendall-Hunt, 1994.

Ruben, B. D. "The Quality Approach in Higher Education: Context and Concepts for Change." In B. D. Ruben (ed.), *Quality in Higher Education.* New Brunswick, N.J.: Transaction, 1995.

Ruben, B. D. *Excellence in Higher Education: A Guide to Organizational Assessment, Planning and Improvement.* Washington, D.C.: National Association of College and University Business Officers, 2000a.

Ruben, B. D. *Excellence in Higher Education: Organizational Assessment, Planning and Improvement Workbook.* Washington, D.C.: National Association of College and University Business Officers, 2000b.

Ruben, B. D. *Excellence in Higher Education: Organizational Assessment, Planning and Improvement Facilitator's Guide and Case Study.* Washington, D.C.: National Association of College and University Business Officers, 2000c.

Ruben, B. D. *Excellence in Higher Education: A Baldrige-Based Guide to Organizational Assessment, Planning and Improvement.* Washington, D.C.: National Association of College and University Business Officers, 2001a.

Ruben, B. D. *Excellence in Higher Education: A Baldrige-Based Organizational Assessment, Planning and Improvement Workbook.* Washington, D.C.: National Association of College and University Business Officers, 2001b.

Ruben, B. D. "We Need Excellence Beyond the Classroom." *Chronicle of Higher Education,* July 13, 2001c, pp. B15–16.

Ruben, B. D. *Excellence in Higher Education: A Baldrige-Based Guide to Organizational Assessment, Improvement and Leadership.* Washington, D.C.: National Association of College and University Business Officers, 2003a.

Ruben, B. D. *Excellence in Higher Education: A Baldrige-Based Guide to Organizational Assessment, Improvement and Leadership. Workbook and Scoring Guide.* Washington, D.C.: National Association of College and University Business Officers, 2003b.

Ruben, B. D. *Excellence in Higher Education 2003–2004: Facilitator's Guide.* Washington, D.C.: National Association of College and University Business Officers, 2003c.

Ruben, B. D. *Pursuing Excellence in Higher Education: Eight Fundamental Challenges.* San Francisco: Jossey-Bass, 2004.

Ruben, B. D. *Excellence in Higher Education: An Integrated Approach to Assessment, Planning and Improvement for Colleges and Universities.* Washington, D.C.: National Association of College and University Business Officers, 2005a.

Ruben, B. D. *Excellence in Higher Education: An Integrated Approach to Assessment, Planning and Improvement for Colleges and Universities. Workbook and Scoring Guide.* Washington, D.C.: National Association of College and University Business Officers, 2005b.

Ruben, B. D. *Excellence in Higher Education: An Integrated Approach to Assessment, Planning and Improvement for Colleges and Universities. Facilitator's Guide.* Washington, D.C.: National Association of College and University Business Officers, 2005c.

Ruben, B. D. "Linking Accreditation Standards and the Malcolm Baldrige Framework: An Integrated Approach to Continuous Assessment, Planning and Improvement." Paper presented at the annual conference of the Middle States Commission on Higher Education, Baltimore, Md., 2005d.

Ruben, B. D. *Excellence in Higher Education Guide: An Integrated Approach to Assessment, Planning and Improvement for Colleges and Universities.* Washington, D.C.: National Association of College and University Business Officers (in press), forthcoming a.

Ruben, B. D. *Excellence in Higher Education: An Integrated Approach to Assessment, Planning and Improvement for Colleges and Universities. Workbook and Scoring Manual.* Washington, D.C.: National Association of College and University Business Officers (in press), forthcoming b.

Ruben, B. D. *Excellence in Higher Education: An Integrated Approach to Assessment, Planning and Improvement for Colleges and Universities. Facilitator's Guide.* Washington, D.C.: National Association of College and University Business Officers (in press), forthcoming c.

Ruben, B. D., Connaughton, S. L., and Russ, T. L. "What Impact Does the Baldrige/Excellence in Higher Education Self-Assessment Process Have on Institutional

Effectiveness?" Paper presented at the annual conference of the National Consortium for Continuous Improvement in Higher Education, Baltimore, Md., 2005.

Ruben, B. D., and Lehr, J. *Excellence in Higher Education: A Guidebook for Self-Assessment, Strategic Planning and Improvement in Higher Education*. Dubuque, Iowa: Kendall-Hunt, 1997a.

Ruben, B. D., and Lehr, J. *Excellence in Higher Education: A Workbook for Self-Assessment, Strategic Planning and Improvement in Higher Education*. Dubuque, Iowa: Kendall-Hunt, 1997b.

Ruben, B. D., Connaughton, S. L., Immordino, K. and Lopez, J. (2004). *What Impact Does the Baldrige/Excellence in Higher Education Self-Assessment Process Have on Institutional Effectiveness?* Preliminary Research Findings. Annual Conference of the National Consortium for Continuous Improvement in Higher Education, Milwaukee, WI, July, 2004.

Ruben, B. D., Russ, T., Smulowitz, S. M., and Connaughton, S. L. "Evaluating the Impact of Organizational Self-Assessment in Higher Education: The Malcolm Baldrige/Excellence in Higher Education Framework." *Leadership and Organizational Development Journal*, 2006.

Schray, V. *Issue Paper 14: Assuring Quality in Higher Education*. Secretary of Education's Commission on the Future of Higher Education, 2006. Retrieved Sept. 1, 2006, from http://www.ed.gov/about/bdscomm/list/hiedfuture/reports/schray2.pdf.

Selingo, J. "Businesses Say They Turn to For-Profit Schools Because of Public Colleges' Inertia." *Chronicle of Higher Education*, July 14, 1999. Retrieved Aug. 20, 1999, from http://chronicle.com/daily/99/07/99071401n.htm.

Seymour, D. T. *On Q: Causing Quality in Higher Education*. New York: American Council on Education and Macmillan, 1989.

Southern Association of Colleges and Schools. Commission on Colleges. *Handbook for Reaffirmation of Accreditation*. Decatur, Ga.: Commission on Colleges, 2003. Retrieved Dec. 15, 2003, from www.sacscoc.org/principles.asp.

Spangehl, S. D. "Aligning Assessment, Academic Quality, and Accreditation." *Assessment and Accountability Forum*, 2000, *10*(2), 10–11, 19.

Spangehl, S. D. "Talking with Academia About Quality—The North Central Association of Colleges and Schools, Academic Quality Improvement Project." In B. D. Ruben (ed.), *Pursuing Excellence in Higher Education: Eight Fundamental Challenges*. San Francisco: Jossey-Bass, 2004.

Spellings Commission. *Final Report-Draft*. Commission on the Future of Higher Education, 2006a. Retrieved Aug. 9, 2006, from http://www.ed.gov/about/bdscomm/list/hiedfuture/reports/0809-draft.pdf.

Spellings Commission. *A National Dialogue: The Secretary of Education's Commission on the Future of Higher Education*. Commission on the Future of Higher Education, 2006b. Retrieved Sept. 1, 2006, from http://www.ed.gov/about/bdscomm/list/hiedfuture/index.html.

Terenzini, P. T., and Pascarella, E. T. "Living with Myths: Undergraduate Education in America." *Change*, 1994, *26*(1), 28–32.

U.S. Department of Education. Archived Video Webcast. Commission on the Future of Higher Education, Apr 6–7, 2006. Retrieved September 1, 2006, from http://www.connectlive.com/events/highered0406/.

Vokurka, R. J. "The Baldrige at 14." *Journal for Quality and Participation*, 2001, *24*(2), 13–19.

Ward, D., and American Council on Education, *President to President*, 2006, *7*(30). Retrieved Sept. 1, 2006, from http://www.acenet.edu/Content/NavigationMenu/Government RelationsPublicPolicy/PresidenttoPresident/Default877.htm.

Weinstein, L. A. *Moving a Battleship with Your Bare Hands*. Madison, Wis.: Magna, 1993.

Western Association of Schools and Colleges. 2004. *How to Become Accredited*. Retrieved Jan. 24, 2007, from http://www.wascsenior.org/wasc/PDFs/HowtoBecome AccreditedManual8.4.06.pdf.

Wilson, D. D., and Collier, D. A. "An Empirical Investigation of the Malcolm Baldrige National Quality Award Causal Model." *Decision Sciences,* 2000, *31*(2), 361–383.

Wilson, R. "It's 10 A.M. Do You Know Where Your Professors Are?" *Chronicle of Higher Education,* Feb. 2, 2001. Retrieved Feb. 15, 2001, from http://chronicle.com/free/v47/i21/21a01001.htm.

Wingspread Group on Higher Education. *An American Imperative: Higher Expectations for Higher Education.* Racine, Wis.: Johnson Foundation, 1993.

BRENT D. RUBEN *is Distinguished Professor of Communication at Rutgers University and executive director of the University Center for Organizational Development and Leadership.*

NEW DIRECTIONS FOR HIGHER EDUCATION • DOI: 10.1002/he

6

University administrators can use information technology to drive innovation through focusing institutional purpose and improving business practices.

Information Technology: A Contributor to Innovation in Higher Education

Ted Dodds

That font of all modern knowledge, Wikipedia, defines *innovation* as "the implementation of a new or significantly improved idea, good, service, process or practice that is intended to be useful."

Three key attributes are identified in this definition: implementation, new or significant improvement, and usefulness. In other words, in order for something to be innovative, it has to be put into practice and used, it has to be radically different from or much better than the status quo, and it has to have a beneficial impact. To this last point, it seems reasonable to make explicit what is implied in the definition: that the beneficial impact is on people. An idea or a solution to a problem cannot be innovative unless it satisfies all three of these conditions.

Using this definition and its specific attributes, we consider three broad areas where information technology is a contributor to university innovation:

- Building communities of innovation
- Radically changing institutional processes and practices
- Implementing infrastructure and tools that enable people to excel

New Directions for Higher Education, no. 137, Spring 2007 © Wiley Periodicals, Inc.
Published online in Wiley InterScience (www.interscience.wiley.com) • DOI: 10.1002/he.247

For each of these three areas, I present a corresponding example taken from our experience at the University of British Columbia:

- The e-Strategy Framework
- Using a formal business process redesign methodology
- Comprehensive network infrastructure, tools, and services

Curiously, only one of these examples might be considered truly technical: the network infrastructure. The simple truth is that technology by itself seldom drives innovation. Rather, it is the combination of factors—building communities of innovation, process change, technology tools—that can energize innovation at a university.

Building Communities of Innovation

Universities comprise communities. There are communities of researchers: teams of people engaged in the exciting prospect of knowledge discovery. There are communities of education: people who share with each other new ideas for effective teaching and learning. Communities of staff exist, sometimes in self-organized groups that gather informally to discuss mutual challenges and solutions. And of course there are students, who have nearly limitless ways of forming social, learning, athletic, virtual, and other types of communities.

What about communities of innovation? How can they be nurtured and sustained? Without suggesting that there is a formula or a single way of doing so, it is reasonable to consider several factors and associated action steps that can foster the development of communities of innovation.

Remove Barriers to Effectiveness. Imagine driving your car with one foot on the gas pedal and one foot on the brake. If you take your foot off the brake, your car will accelerate without your having to press harder on the gas. Removing barriers to effectiveness is like lifting your foot off the brake pedal: you will accelerate without expending more energy.

Institutions can find ways of systematically reducing the amount of low-value work people do so that they can focus on more important activities. The notion of removing barriers to effectiveness is closely linked to the later discussion on business process innovation.

By eliminating unnecessary steps in a process, such as reducing signatures and multiple checkpoints required to approve simple transactions, or by reengineering the old process entirely, we can give people the precious gift of time. Researchers can focus on research, not on the administration of research. Staff can spend less time enforcing rules and more time providing personalized service. Students can access the services they need when and where they need them.

No researcher wins a Nobel prize for administering research. No student gets an A for standing in line.

NEW DIRECTIONS FOR HIGHER EDUCATION • DOI: 10.1002/he

Create Effective Services and New Possibilities for Collaboration. One of the most important areas where information technology (IT) can contribute to innovation is through infrastructure and services that enable collaboration. Envision interdisciplinary research without ubiquitous networks. Consider the astonishingly rapid uptake in learning management systems that enable professors and students to take learning beyond the classroom. And for all the complaints we hear about the daily avalanche of e-mails, think how this service has transformed the workplace and increased the pace at which we work.

Effective IT-enabled services at a university have certain key characteristics that make them great contributors to innovation. They scale from small to large so that they are available to everyone who needs to use them. They are secure and easy to use, and they require no specialized training. The services support local configuration and optimization without losing their institutionwide effectiveness. The campus network is an excellent example of IT infrastructure and services that have these attributes.

Establish Continuous Communication. One of the delightful qualities of a community is its enjoyment of coming together in discussion, debate, and information sharing. Universities, particularly large research-intensive ones like the University of British Columbia, present inherent, though unintentional, obstacles to communication. In my experience, it takes effort to gather people together, physically or virtually. It is not easy to keep people informed.

Periodic events such as interactive town hall meetings can be designed to keep the community informed and engaged. Existing technologies such as podcasts, wikis, blogs, and electronic newsletters with reader feedback forums built in can go a long way to keeping that sense of engagement and involvement. They enhance collaboration and retain the flow of information so that people know who is doing what and can celebrate mutual success.

Trust People. Creating a culture of trust, demonstrating empowerment to staff and faculty, can be encouraged or discouraged by the nature of IT systems. Consider the fact that taxpayers can file their annual returns online while retaining paper receipts for a specified period in case they are required. In taking this approach in its systems, the tax department conveys implicit trust in taxpayers. It assumes people will fill in their return correctly and accurately and will not cheat. Clearly it must have back-end systems designed to pick up irregularities that may require follow-up, but it deals with the exceptions only.

Compare this to a university process as simple as travel claims. At many institutions, these transactions entail astonishing levels of detailed paper records submitted at the time of claim. A series of steps of verification and checking occurs. It is not unusual to see an original claim that has been altered by very slight amounts, indicating that someone has taken the time and trouble to recalculate sums and make minor corrections. This is the opposite of assuming honesty in the people using a system. All transactions, not just the exceptions, are scrutinized. Processes like this do not lead to innovation. The sense of being micromanaged is one that rankles faculty and staff. Why can the tax department do it right and we cannot?

This idea speaks to a particular vision and set of values that places conservative university culture at odds with the creation of a virtuous cycle of trust and empowerment that can drive innovation, creativity, and optimism.

Start with the Vision. Ever since UBC launched its e-Strategy Framework in 2001, an important part of our vision has been to change what people mean when they utter the phrase, "That's how we do things around here." More often than not, these words lament the great complexity and impenetrable bureaucracy that can sometimes be found in any university and are the antithesis of innovation.

Our basic premise is that the institution is full of intelligent, committed people whose potential to excel can be either enhanced or reduced by internal processes and practices and the usability of IT infrastructure and tools. Therefore, to help create communities of innovation within the university, we aspire to give people the time, tools, and processes they need to excel.

We believe IT can foster a culture of innovation by taking the point of view of the individual. Technical people might call this a user-centric perspective, as contrasted with either a techno-centric or a department-centric view. It might seem self-evident to most people that IT solutions should be designed with the end user in mind. Yet surprisingly this is often not the case. In the decentralized environments that characterize institutions, it can be exceedingly difficult to entice solution providers to think beyond that which is of benefit to their own unit and consider the university as a whole.

UBC does not have a formal strategic plan for IT. What we do have is the e-Strategy Framework, which generally mirrors the five pillars of UBC's institution-level strategic vision: People, Learning, Research, Community, and Internationalization. The e-Strategy provides an organizing and guiding framework for IT-related issues, ideas, and initiatives.

The e-Strategy Framework was launched at a town hall meeting held in 2001. University president Martha Piper opened the meeting by explaining the importance of a shared vision. The vision, she said, is like the picture on the box-top cover of a jigsaw puzzle. Each of us has a different way of putting together the pieces of the puzzle, yet we all need to refer to the same picture on the cover; otherwise, the puzzle will remain unfinished.

The e-Strategy town hall is now an annual event. It is an opportunity for the community to meet, discuss, learn, interact, and have fun. We believe it is an important aspect of our drive for excellence and innovation because it builds and rebuilds the community. Like any other good conference, most of the important work is done between the formal sessions: people talking to people.

The e-Strategy has helped improve IT governance. All five of the university's vice presidents have responsibility for systems and technology within their portfolio. By pulling together all of the vice presidents in the e-Strategy

New Directions for Higher Education • DOI: 10.1002/he

executive steering committee, we are able to present the executive group with a consolidated list of IT priorities that spans the five portfolios. Simple as it sounds, this small step has served to increase mutual understanding of IT priorities that did not exist previously. It has enabled us to reach consensus on some large IT investments. As it approaches its fifth birthday, we are overhauling the e-Strategy governance processes and structures.

IT governance is connected to innovation by ensuring that we are allocating scarce IT resources to areas of greatest and highest potential benefit; by asking and answering the question of who contributes to IT decision making; and by raising the bar from local optimization to the level of the institution. A shared vision and improved IT decision making have led to significant new investments in IT infrastructure and systems.

I believe UBC's e-Strategy Framework reflects the three attributes in the definition of innovation: it has been implemented, it is a significant improvement over what existed before, and it is a benefit to people. That said, we have a long and challenging road before us.

New or Significantly Improved Processes: Beyond Best Practice

Ask yourself to what degree the business and academic processes at your institution reflect purposeful design rather than ad hoc evolution over time. In my experience, there are many more examples of the latter than the former. By strategically redesigning core university processes, we can unlock radical changes, improve the way things get done, and thereby drive innovation.

Changing a business process is not the same as implementing a new IT system. Processes typically span multiple domains within an institution. Information flow in a business process is horizontal, moving across and through administrative borders. By contrast, the majority of existing software systems were designed to automate particular functions, often reflecting departmental boundaries, which themselves are only a portion of an overall process. Information flow in many of the systems in place today is vertical.

Consider the example of a student information system (SIS). It supports business functions in the registrar's office, such as registering students and collecting tuition payments. However, many of these systems do not allow a student to make payments that are not related to functions in the registrar's office, such as library fines, parking fees, or buying textbooks. By contrast, a student needs to pay the bills, no matter which university department might be involved. In short, existing systems tend to be oriented to the needs of the department, not to the needs of the end user.

In addition to lacking the user's perspective on business process, most commercial systems require the institution to modify its existing practices to accommodate the system. This is often viewed as a better option than modifying a complex software package to match current processes because modifications could lead to expensive maintenance of the software, and commercial software products are designed around a set of best practices that are encoded in the software. If an institution were to modify best practice software and instead encode the current ad hoc business processes, it would be forgoing an opportunity for positive change. At least, that is the theory.

But what if an institution employed a combination of strategically planned process redesign together with the newly emerging IT platforms that are designed to operate as services rather than as monolithic application systems? As communities, we would then have the ability to create and implement through software our own practices rather than an abstract notion of best practices.

Would such an approach lead to greater innovation? In areas where an institution seeks differentiation from its competitors and peers, the answer is yes. By designing and then implementing its own business processes through easily configurable service-oriented software, a university can tailor its relationship with students and alumni, reflect unique aspects of its own research capabilities and goals, and save all members of the community valuable time.

There are other cases—payroll processing, for example, where the best practice approach makes the most sense. Universities do not typically rely on the payroll system to be a strategic differentiator as long as it pays people accurately and on time.

Over the past several years, many units across our campus have used a structured methodology for business process redesign (BPR). The methodology was introduced to us by JM Associates, a small higher education–focused consulting firm.

Based on the Hammer-Champy (1993) approach but modified for higher education, the methodology scales well. It is effective in creating small changes by streamlining existing processes. More exciting is its capacity to radically reinvent large core processes such as student admission and employee recruitment and hiring, both of which have been reengineered at UBC using this methodology.

A case for action is developed illustrating why the process needs to change. A steering committee approves a statement of the desired end result that describes the desired outcome of the redesigned process. The redesign team is given the statement of the end result and is required to create a business process to achieve it. The end result tells the team what the process outcome should be; it is the team's job to figure out how the process should work.

Smaller streamlining efforts typically take two to three weeks to complete the redesign phase. Larger redesigns may last eight to ten weeks. Each redesign team has six to ten people working full time through the redesign phase. Clearly BPR is not without cost. However, the benefits can be dramatic.

The most powerful aspect of the methodology is its reliability. A team that follows the methodology is virtually guaranteed to create a redesigned process that satisfies the statement of end results that is agreed to up front.

We have found that people who participate in a redesign team are changed by the experience. They continue to play the role of change agents when they return to their regular responsibilities. They continue to question current practices and look for ways to improve on the status quo.

Radical change requires strong leadership. UBC has been fortunate to have such leadership at the highest level, including the president and several vice presidents. Our vice president of students was the executive sponsor of a BPR that transformed the experience of incoming UBC students (including the ability for students to self-assess and admit themselves on the Web, as well as a service known as consolidated billing that provides a one-stop financial statement). Our vice president of administration and finance was executive sponsor of a BPR entitled Enabling Opportunities that radically redesigned the processes around employee recruitment, hiring, and ongoing employee engagement.

Returning to the definition of innovation, business process redesign at UBC has clearly resulted in new or significantly improved process designs that are useful to people. For us, implementation remains the biggest challenge. Although the methodology is almost guaranteed, the transition from redesign to implementation is not. Having struggled with this challenge ourselves, we have recommended the establishment of an ongoing program of BPR that would include a reserve set aside for implementation (planning and initial deployment of the new process).

Implementing IT Infrastructure and Tools That Enable People to Excel

University excellence is a product of people—faculty, students, and staff—who play differing roles in the pursuit of scholarship and learning. Excellence is not a product of technology. However, the implementation of new IT-based services or applications can play a direct role in enabling people to excel through simple time-saving tools and reliable infrastructure.

As organizations, universities often are characterized by distributed decision making, a high degree of local autonomy within academic units, and decentralized resource allocation. Yet surrounding these distributed activities is the broader fabric of the institution itself.

The campus network is an excellent example of IT infrastructure that makes a profound impact on innovation, in part by mirroring the organizational attributes of a university (autonomy and decentralization within a broader fabric). The network is a single comprehensive example of a research and learning infrastructure that permeates the institution. If it is properly carried out, the nature of network design will make it reliable and scalable and should offer a high degree of localized control, without local configuration and use decisions interfering with the work environment of others.

Consider the data network's impact on research innovation. The human dimension of contemporary research has changed from the lone scholar in the so-called ivory tower to international multidisciplinary teams of investigators. Research is now fundamentally data driven rather than direct observation driven. Data-driven research dominates all areas of research, from the life and physical sciences to new applications in the humanities and social sciences. An unprecedented amount of research data is generated each day, data that need to be accessed, manipulated, stored, archived, managed, and visualized.

Network infrastructure is at the core of a complex array of technologies that enable research innovation. The network contributes to the success of investigators in literally all disciplines. In short, leading-edge research requires leading-edge networks. In Canada, CANARIE Inc., a semi-private corporation dedicated to accelerating the nation's advanced Internet development, has designed and deployed four generations of advanced networks that foster innovation locally and internationally. By giving the research community universal access to data, equipment, and colleagues around the world, the network increases the institution's ability to attract funding, partnerships, and high-quality people.

One of the first and most important steps any university can take toward becoming more innovative is to ensure it has the finest networking connectivity possible. This requires connections on campus, in affiliated research and teaching spaces, and across regional and national borders.

Contemporary research networks, on campus or at a national level, are reaching beyond wires and blinking lights. Increasingly, it is the suite of services or tools that are directly linked to the network that give researchers new capabilities and control over their environment. These tools enable researchers to excel and innovate.

The growing suite of network-based tools includes some exciting developments. It is increasingly easy for a researcher to access remote scientific equipment or other research resources, no matter where they are in the world, by means of optical light paths: secure, high-speed, point-to-point connections that connect directly to a remote resource. Researchers thus can link the research team with needed resources.

A lack of sophisticated research equipment within a particular department or campus can now be overcome by accessing facilities elsewhere in the world. Whereas this lack of campus-based resources may have constrained the very research questions that could be considered, globally accessible resources open up powerful new avenues for innovation.

At the completion of a major upgrade project in 2003, UBC's network infrastructure included twenty-five thousand wired ports, twelve hundred wireless access points, and optical connectivity to regional and national research networks. By June 2006, the overall capacity measured by the number of wired ports had doubled to fifty thousand. We will reach two thousand wireless access points during 2007. Over twenty thousand people use the wireless network on a regular basis, with four thousand of those online at a given moment. Those figures continue to climb. There are two thousand voice-over-Internet-protocol connections. Our network planning today is based on one integrated infrastructure that will carry data, voice, and video.

NEW DIRECTIONS FOR HIGHER EDUCATION • DOI: 10.1002/he

Part of the growth in the size of the network is driven by the growth of the university itself. But beyond mere numbers, there are important links to academic innovation. In 2004, for example, the University of British Columbia's Faculty of Medicine successfully launched an innovative, distributed M.D. undergraduate program in collaboration with the government of British Columbia, the University of Northern British Columbia, the University of Victoria, and the provincial regional health authorities. The first of its kind in Canada, the program has created new opportunities for medical education across British Columbia and will double the number of M.D. graduates by 2010. The purpose of the program is to increase access for the public to physicians in both urban and rural areas across the province and improve the health of its residents.

Advanced networking and network-based services such as videoconferencing and collaboration are vital to this innovative program. Accreditation status for our M.D. program is now inextricably linked with information technology and the network first and foremost.

Our deployment of wireless networking on campus dates to 2002. We made a conscious decision at that time to make the network as easy to access and use as possible, even if in so doing we made the network slightly less secure. There were risks in this approach, but we felt they were worth taking. Our goal, and the project's indicator of success, was rapid adoption of the new wireless network. That is precisely what happened. As a result of widespread adoption of a new tool, faculty and students had more opportunities for collaboration, communication, and interaction.

UBC's wireless network provides ubiquitous mobility for all researchers and is enabling collaboration on demand. Impromptu research collaboration and brainstorming need to support online simulations, file transfer, and reduced latency response (for mobile videoconferencing). Current wireless technology cannot cope with these demands, so we are planning for next-generation wireless networking in order to keep fueling the fires of innovation.

Exemplifying the ability to provide local control within a single fabric of institutional infrastructure, UBC's homegrown tool known as the transmogrifier has revolutionized network support by empowering local departmental network managers to troubleshoot, control, configure, and document their own network areas. Network managers in numerous university departments throughout UBC log in to the transmogrifier using a secure Web site on a day-to-day basis to turn ports on or off, configure their own virtual local networks, view statistics, and document relevant information. Our next steps will be giving researchers direct use of tools like the transmogrifier so that they can manage many more aspects of their research environment.

So, to return again to the three defined attributes of innovation, networks are nearly everywhere (they are implemented), universities have gone from little connectivity to optical light paths (new or significantly improved), and the community cannot function effectively without them (useful to people). Networks drive innovation in our universities.

Next Steps in IT-Driven Innovation

Here are many exciting trends in information technology and numerous new possibilities. Three of these stand out in the context of this discussion of innovation: systems comprising services, community source software, and next-generation Internet tools. Together they represent a promising combination for future IT-driven innovation.

Systems Comprising Services. The majority of existing commercial and internally developed systems tend to reflect a departmental rather than a business process orientation. They are often described as integrated, which unfortunately can mean monolithic.

That is changing and likely to change quite significantly in the next several years. Developments in service-oriented architecture (SOA) are based on the principle that systems of loosely coupled standardized services will be more flexible, less costly to maintain, and more reliable to use. In this context, a service could be "process a credit card payment" or "set up a light path."

Services communicate with one another through open standard protocols. They all speak the same language. Rather than customizing complex software packages, people can configure services to interact in ways that reflect their needs. A service-oriented IT architecture holds the promise of truly liberating us from best practice to our practice.

As promising as it is from a technology perspective, the biggest challenge we are likely to have with SOA will be organizational and cultural. We will have tools and systems capable of leaping departmental borders, but people will need to agree to use them, knowing that the new tools threaten to erode the clandestinely cherished departmental silos.

Community Source Software. Complementary to the principles of SOA is the burgeoning community (open) source movement. In the IT industry, open source products such as Linux, a computer operating system, are made freely available to those who wish to use them. New business models, based on free software but for-fee support services, have altered the competitive landscape.

In higher education, the Java Architectures Special Interest Group (JA-SIG) has nurtured the development of several community source products. One of these is uPortal, a Web portal framework in use by hundreds of universities worldwide. In important ways, JA-SIG helped lay the foundation for other successful community source projects, notably Sakai, in the arena of learning management and collaboration, and Kuali, a financial management application. A feasibility study is under way to determine if the time is right to create a next-generation service-oriented student system.

There are a great many other community source projects and products in use at universities. The number and size of open source projects will

NEW DIRECTIONS FOR HIGHER EDUCATION • DOI: 10.1002/he

continue to grow and exert positive influence on the software industry. The result, whether decision makers opt for open source or proprietary software for any particular system, is that our communities have more choice and more voice.

The open source movement is itself a form of management innovation. It has proven to be a very effective means of coordinating the efforts of geographically and organizationally dispersed teams.

Next-Generation Tools. We are beginning to see a new generation of IT tools that are designed for the Internet rather than the computer. These tools are already enabling people to harness more of the power of the network than ever before. The fundamental notion behind this new generation of tools is collaboration, reuse and recombination of existing services in novel ways, and leveraging the power of the Internet.

Unfortunately, like many other technical innovations, the new generation of IT tools comes complete with its own alphabet soup of acronyms and arcane language. Some of these terms, such as business process execution language (BPEL), begin to merge the language of business process and computer programming. The promise of BPEL is its ability to orchestrate multiple services into an overall business process. And then there is AJAX, a group of technologies that increase a Web page's interactivity, speed, and usability. AJAX can give Web sites interactivity features similar to those found in personal computer applications like spreadsheets.

Indeed, a frequently used analogy is the electronic spreadsheet, a tool with which we are all familiar and that put revolutionary new capabilities and power into the hands of end users. As a tool, the spreadsheet is remarkably flexible: nontechnical people can use it for everything from managing their personal finances to tracking the results of an athletic competition.

Conclusion

Information technology can and should be expected to contribute to innovation in university life. IT makes this contribution in research, learning, administrative activities, and other important areas such as collaboration and community building. By starting with a clear vision, being thoughtful about business practices, and providing excellent IT infrastructure and services, university administrators can create an environment in which innovation can flourish.

Reference

Hammer, M., and Champy, J. *Reengineering the Corporation: A Manifesto for Business Revolution.* New York: HarperBusiness, 1993.

TED DODDS *is the chief information officer and associate vice president for information technology at the University of British Columbia.*

This chapter, drawing from the previous chapters, synthesizes potential directions and implications of future innovation in higher education. The focus is on innovation to address critical issues that administrators face today: the adaptability, maturity, cost structure, and efficiency of the institution.

Innovation in Higher Education: Implications for the Future

Susan C. White, Theodore S. Glickman

In common parlance, the term *innovation* refers to the introduction of a new idea, method, or device. From a management perspective, Peter Drucker suggested that innovation is a "change that creates a new dimension of performance" (Hesselbein, Goldsmith, and Somerville, 2002, p. xi), and from an institutional perspective, as put forth by the U.K. Department of Trade and Industry, innovation is the successful exploitation of new ideas. The same range of meanings applies in higher education, where innovation can refer simply to some new way of doing things, or a change that improves administrative or scholarly performance, or a transformational experience based on a new way of thinking. Today's higher education administrators, who must balance the fiscal pressures of running a large organization influenced by external forces such as rankings and increased competition for students and faculty and internal stresses produced by boards and accrediting agencies who are demanding more transparency, accountability, and tangible evidence of success, are best served by seeking continued innovation in curricular programs, delivery mechanisms, support services, and operations. In this volume, we have presented ideas for new ways of conducting business within the context of higher education. These, and more, are crucial to the continued success of institutions of higher learning.

Innovation can offer flexibility to enable institutions to adapt more readily in a constantly changing environment, a means by which colleges and universities can address concerns typically associated with mature

NEW DIRECTIONS FOR HIGHER EDUCATION, no. 137, Spring 2007 © Wiley Periodicals, Inc.
Published online in Wiley InterScience (www.interscience.wiley.com) • DOI: 10.1002/he.248

enterprises, tools to ease increasing cost pressures, and efficiency gains through better operations and better matching of resources and requirements. Each of these benefits is addressed in this chapter.

Innovation and Flexibility

Higher education continues to evolve worldwide. From the origination of Plato's Academy in ancient Greece, to the founding of Oxford's University College in 1249 A.D., to the legislation for land grant universities in the United States through the Morrill Act of 1862, up to the advent of online degree programs in the late twentieth century, the landscape in higher education has been constantly changing. While this evolution has led to the expansion of the higher education industry and advancement in educational aspirations and attainment, ongoing improvement in these dimensions is imperative. As cited in the recent Spellings Report (U.S. Department of Education, 2006, p. vii), "this new landscape demands innovation and flexibility."

In this volume, we have examined some ways in which higher education is evolving and improving to meet the challenges of the contemporary landscape. These include closer examination of quality, novel uses of technology, ways to reach learners with disabilities, and curricular innovations.

An emphasis on quality, while not necessarily innovative according to the common definition of *innovation* (the introduction of a new idea, method, or device), is innovative in the establishment of ongoing processes to ensure openness and ongoing improvements in higher education administration. In the United States, the Baldrige National Quality Program provides both incentives and a basic framework for examining the procedures in place in higher education institutions to support quality in all facets: curriculum design, instruction, student services, and supporting operations. In Chapter One, Julie Furst-Bowe and Roy Bauer describe how implementing the Baldrige framework at the University of Wisconsin-Stout has helped drive innovation and facilitated sustained improvements. In Chapter Five, Brent Ruben examines the Baldrige framework and focuses on ways in which excellence indicators can be linked to accreditation standards to encourage innovation, excellence, and ongoing gains in operational efficiencies and quality. Institutions must remain flexible so they can benefit from these innovations.

Focusing on technology, Kevin Kinser and Ted Dodds (Chapters Two and Six, respectively) discuss how it can drive innovations in operations and offer opportunities for the delivery of academic programs in novel ways. The flexibility afforded by new technologies can facilitate gains in many facets of an institution's operations, provided that the institutions are willing and able to adopt the technologies.

In Chapter Three, Robbin Zeff discusses the issue of increasing the accessibility of higher education to people with different learning styles and learning disabilities. Universal design for learning (UDL) offers a road map for implementing new technologies, coupled with innovations in the ways in which content is constructed, presented, and delivered. As institutions recognize the broader implications of accessibility as espoused by UDL, they will find potential for improvements in academic and ancillary services.

Curricular innovation, as exhibited by Western Governors University and the Leadership Foundation for Higher Education in the United Kingdom, is a hallmark of innovation and flexibility within the academy, according to Kinser in Chapter Two and Robin Middlehurst in Chapter Four. They discuss initiatives in the United States and United Kingdom that have effected change beyond the confines of one institution. In addition to program development and curricular reform, innovations such as these can help institutions meet standards dictated by accrediting agencies and drive changes in the accrediting processes themselves.

Western Governors University was born out of the desire to offer access to higher education to an increasing number of students in an era of fixed, or even declining, state appropriations for colleges and universities. The competency-based model, which was delivered using a wide variety of instructional methods, conflicted with traditional accrediting processes, including the fundamental tenets of faculty and curriculum development. This truly innovative approach survived the unintended consequences brought about by mechanisms already in place to assess and ensure learning outcomes. This case study also offers some clues to potential challenges to novel approaches.

The lessons gleaned from an examination of the development of the Leadership Foundation for Higher Education include insights into the research, political, and timing issues familiar to those who seek to offer new approaches in curricular and program design. Again, these challenges suggest that flexibility is a necessary condition for successful innovation in higher education. The Baldrige Award also offers learning opportunities for those seeking to develop new curricula and programs. These efforts can be supported by the inclusion of pedagogical reform to address universal accessibility.

Finally, information technology affects not only the delivery of academic content but also ancillary operations. If today's students are more technologically savvy than the majority of the faculty, the implications for the academy surely include a wide range of opportunities to leverage the fruits of new hardware and software tools in ways that truly enhance the learning experience. This will require flexibility on the part of the faculty. In addition, as schools are more ratings conscious, new ways to innovate in the delivery of supporting services will emerge; institutions whose operating processes are most open to change will reap the most benefits.

NEW DIRECTIONS FOR HIGHER EDUCATION • DOI: 10.1002/he

Innovation in a Mature Enterprise

The Spellings Report finds that "American higher education has become what, in the business world, would be called a mature enterprise: increasingly risk-averse, at times self-satisfied, and unduly expensive" (U.S. Department of Education, 2006, p. ix). It is harder to innovate in a mature enterprise. Risk-averse behaviors do not lend themselves to trying new ideas or new ways of operating. Self-satisfaction allows little cause for the reflection that precedes innovation, and fiscal pressures may offer easy excuses to maintain the status quo. The chapters in this volume nevertheless suggest that innovation can and does happen in higher education today.

Unfortunately, this may be a case of too little, too late. The 2006 National Report Card on Higher Education in the United States compares the performance of U.S. colleges and universities to one another and to their counterparts abroad. The bottom line, according to the authors of the report, is that "the current level of performance [in U.S. higher education] will fall short in a world being reshaped by the knowledge-based global economy" (National Center for Public Policy and Higher Education, 2006, p. 5). Completion rates have fallen to the point that the United States ranks in the bottom half (sixteenth among the twenty-seven countries considered) in the proportion of students who complete a college degree or certificate program. In fact, completion rates in Georgia, the best-performing state, fall below those in Japan, Portugal, the United Kingdom, Australia, Switzerland, and Denmark. In the same vein, the Spellings Report notes that "over the past decade, literacy among college graduates has actually declined" (U.S. Department of Education, 2006, p. vii). Not only have costs risen dramatically, but the performance of graduates appears to have declined.

The challenge is to motivate innovation in the mature enterprise that higher education has become. Programs such as the Baldrige Award and initiatives like UDL offer systematic ways to foster and encourage the development of new processes and programs. As presented in this volume, these programs are being implemented in mature institutions, and the institutions are noticing positive benefits.

In contrast, the Spellings Report demands innovation beyond the traditional scope of inputs and processes, finding that institutions must develop innovative ways to demonstrate learning outcomes and measure student performance and learning. In short, the U.S. Department of Education is urging the accreditation community to place greater emphasis on results. While new technologies can assist with the compilation, presentation, and assessment of data, innovation demands new data generated in novel ways that examines the institution from different perspectives. Institutions that have process-oriented programs in place, such as the ones discussed in these chapters, will be better positioned to find new ways of thinking about results.

Nicholas M. Donofrio (2006), executive vice president for innovation and technology at IBM, calls for collaboration—a collaboration of multiple and diverse cultures—to break the malaise. He maintains that innovation has to be more multidisciplinary, with collaboration among experts from many different backgrounds. The effort must include experts and users and requires breaking down barriers and destroying the disciplinary and functional silos that have grown as institutions have matured. This has been demonstrated through the creation of Western Governors University.

Innovation and Cost Pressures

The following quotations paint a bleak picture of rising costs coupled with declining fiscal support for higher education, bringing into question the long-term viability of the current model of higher education funding:

> The Commission notes with concern the seemingly inexorable increase in college costs, which have outpaced inflation for the past two decades and have made affordability an ever-growing worry for students, families, and policymakers. Too many students are either discouraged from attending college by rising costs, or take on worrisome debt burdens in order to do so [U.S. Department of Education, 2006, p. 2].

> Education is supposed to be an equalizer. But with costs rising, students are trading down dreams of an Ivy League education for one at a state university, and from a state university to one at a community college. While all education will bear fruit, we are creating a bifurcated system in which the best education will go to those who can pay for it. Students of color and those of modest means will most likely be the ones left behind [Malveaux, 2006].

> External support for major academic innovation in colleges and universities has significantly decreased in the past decade. State and federal per capita funding has decreased, a number of major foundations have shifted their priorities away from higher education, and business and industry have changed their focus to supporting only those projects that are seen as having an immediate and positive beneficial impact on their bottom line [Diamond, 2006].

The chapters in this volume offer some potential solutions to these concerns. The model laid out by the founders of Western Governors University shows promise in the area of fiscal restraint. Similarly, Rio Salado College in Arizona has about thirty full-time faculty overseeing approximately a thousand adjuncts who teach the 46,800 for-credit students and 14,000 non-degree-seeking students. The question that must be asked of this model goes to the fundamental tenet of a university: the creation and dissemination of knowledge. While adjuncts can disseminate knowledge and assessments can measure students' performance, skills, and abilities, this new model offers little in the way to support traditional research, which is germane to the academy. At the time of this writing, the recipients of the 2006 Nobel prizes for chemistry, physics, and medicine had just been

NEW DIRECTIONS FOR HIGHER EDUCATION • DOI: 10.1002/he

named. They all are affiliated with U.S. universities. Some have claimed that the U.S. model of research better fosters discoveries like those made by the 2006 Nobel laureates. The tension between fiscal restraint and basic research will be difficult to address.

Universal design for learning has cost-based implications. Whether academic or cocurricular, programs that are designed using UDL principles are meant to be accessible and available to a broad and diverse audience. Rather than having to undergo costly redesigns or retrofitting after the fact, innovation that employs UDL from inception is inherently predisposed to be more inclusive and more accessible without being more costly. Of course, in mature institutions, faculty, administrators, and staff should continually look for ways to revise current processes to be more inclusive; it is likely that staff members—those closest to the end users—will have the most direct contact with the people who are most directly affected by the processes. Hence, it is vital that staff members, and everyone else who has close contact with users, feel that their suggestions for innovation will be heard.

IT innovations can support UDL and other new programs and initiatives. New technology typically comes with a higher price tag than administrators hope to see. However, the potential efficiency gains that can be realized with efficient and effective deployment can offset the initial expense and help achieve more attractive cost structures in the long term. These innovations must be managed to take advantage of the continuous refinements and improvement in the hardware and software itself while not being perpetually postponed awaiting the introduction of the next generation.

Institutions that have implemented formal processes to monitor operations and seek improvements, such as those that have participated in the Baldrige Award program, understand the simple steps required for continuous review: (1) examine a key process carefully and thoughtfully; (2) document the process to ensure that all parties have the same understanding of its operation and goals; (3) develop meaningful metrics to measure process outcomes in relation to its goals, and determine baseline measures; (4) look for ways to improve the process; (5) implement selected improvements; (6) compare measurements after the improvements with the baseline measures; (7) if the process shows improvement, document the changes; and (8) repeat the process. This continuous review process is not necessarily expensive, but it can be costly to ignore.

Innovation and Efficiency

"While students bear the immediate brunt of tuition increases, affordability is also a crucial policy dilemma for those who are asked to fund higher education, notably federal and state taxpayers. Even as institutional costs go up, state subsidies are decreasing and public concern about affordability may eventually contribute to an erosion of confidence in higher education. In our view, affordability is directly affected by a financing system that provides limited incentives for colleges and universities to take aggressive steps to improve institutional efficiency and productivity" (U.S. Department of Education, 2006, p. 2).

Productivity is the ratio of outputs to inputs. The fundamental output of higher education is knowledge, whether it is new knowledge discovered through basic research conducted by faculty and students or the knowledge transferred from faculty to students and from faculty to society at large. As our knowledge base grows (that is, our numerator shows gains), the overall productivity ratio must increase if the cost of the inputs—facilities, faculty salaries, support staff, and ancillary programs—holds steady or declines (that is, the funding remains constant or drops). In short, institutions of higher education must exhibit productivity gains to survive in the current environment. Universities must continually seek ways to innovate and thereby deliver increased productivity through gains in operating efficiencies. Institutions have sought such improvements in several ways: outsourcing of ancillary services, developing consortia to support a broad variety of academic programs, using technology better, and matching inputs and outputs more closely.

The outsourcing of ancillary services is not necessarily innovative in today's environment. Typically universities have outsourced a wide variety of services, including food services, vending, bookstore operations, custodial services, maintenance services, and laundry services. In addition, facilities management and administrative services may be outsourced. Outsourcing of these ancillary services allows the institutions to focus on the primary functions of the creation and dissemination of knowledge, their core competency. As universities continue to look for ways to increase operating efficiencies, it is possible that more services will be outsourced. In a sense, that is what is happening at Western Governors University, where the assessment of existing knowledge, skills, and abilities has replaced classroom instruction to an extent.

Consortia are another means by which institutions of higher learning can outsource courses and degree programs. In areas where several universities are geographically close, schools may choose to focus most of their resources on a selected group of academic disciplines. If the schools work together, students may enroll in one institution and take the classes needed to fulfill academic requirements or personal inquiry from all the schools in the consortium. This system allows the participating schools to maintain more universal offerings without bearing the burden of fiscal support for diverse programs.

Technology now allows consortia to extend beyond traditional geographical boundaries. Not only can consortia benefit from technology, but with the judicious use of technological innovations, institutions can become more efficient while remaining responsive to environmental changes. The past twenty years have witnessed rapid changes in record keeping, ranging from degree audits and transcripts to course registration and the payment of tuition and fees. This trend toward the increasing use of technology is making its presence known in the classroom, as evidenced by mandatory laptop computers for all students and the introduction of iPods to the curriculum. In order to realize a greater proportion of the potential benefits of new technology, it is vital that institutions reexamine their processes to make the most efficient and effective use of technology. In many cases, a class taught in the technology classroom is not much different from a class taught using a lectern and a chalkboard. If this is the case, then the technology has merely added bells and whistles at great cost. Faculty may have to reinvent themselves to make the most effective use of the available technologies.

Finally, a better matching of inputs and outputs will lead to greater efficiencies. At innovative institutions, this might mean that students access tutorials prior to enrolling in a course in order to achieve more homogeneous background preparation. Faculty can use technology to receive immediate feedback during a class meeting; this feedback will allow the faculty member to focus on areas in which the students exhibit the least understanding and not expend too much time or energy on topics where students demonstrate a greater depth of knowledge. A better matching of inputs and outputs might also mean better scheduling of extracurricular activities given student input using technology.

Final Thoughts

The challenges facing higher education today are both new and familiar. Flexibility, maturity, fiscal responsibility, and efficiency gains are not innovative in and of themselves. However, the shrinking world in which we live, which journalist Thomas Friedman (2006) refers to as the flat and highly interconnected world of the twenty-first century, brings new insight and urgency to these issues. Although a single volume cannot address every concern, the thought-provoking chapters here will provide an impetus for the next round of innovations in the areas of institutional processes, program design, the application of technology in many facets of an institution's operations, and curricular evolution. It is up to each of us to continue this conversation. If we do not, some of our foremost schools may not survive to see the dawn of the twenty-second century.

References

Diamond, R. M. "Why Colleges Are So Hard to Change." *Inside Higher Ed*, Sept. 8, 2006. Retrieved Oct. 15, 2006, from http://www.insidehighered.com/views /2006/09/08/ diamond.

Donofrio, N. M. "An Engine for Innovation." *Diverse Issues in Higher Education*, 2006, 23(2), 45. Retrieved Jan. 24, 2007, from www.diverseeducation.com/artman/ publish/printer_5576.shtml.

Friedman, T. L. *The World Is Flat: A Brief History of the Twenty-First Century*. New York: Strauss and Giroux, 2006.

Hesselbein, F., Goldsmith, M., and Somerville, I. (eds.). *Leading for Innovation and Organizing for Results*. San Francisco: Jossey-Bass, 2002.

Malveaux, J. "Rising College Fees Will Cost Us in Time." *USA Today*, Aug. 17, 2006. Retrieved Aug. 20, 2006, from http://www.usatoday.com/news/opinion/editorials/2006–08–17-malveaux-edit_x.htm.

National Center for Public Policy and Higher Education. *Measuring Up 2006: The National Report Card on Higher Education*. San Jose, Calif.: National Center for Public Policy and Higher Education, 2006. Retrieved Sept. 15, 2006, from http://higher education.org.

U.S. Department of Education. *A Test of Leadership: Charting the Future of U.S. Higher Education: A Report of the Commission Appointed by Secretary of Education Margaret Spellings*. Washington, D.C: U.S. Government Printing Office, 2006.

SUSAN C. WHITE *is assistant professor of decision sciences in the Business School at George Washington University and co-deputy director of Writing in the Disciplines.*

THEODORE S. GLICKMAN *is associate professor of decision sciences in the George Washington University Business School and senior fellow in the Homeland Security Policy Institute.*

NEW DIRECTIONS FOR HIGHER EDUCATION • DOI: 10.1002/he

INDEX

Academic life cults, 51
Academic Quality Improvement Program (AQIP), 7
Accessibility for Ontarians and Disabilities Act (2005), 40
Accreditation: Baldrige Award Program linked to, 76–77; Baldrige National Quality Award impact on, 2, 7–8; reflective review of higher education, 63–65; of Western Governors University, 16–17, 18–19. *See also* Higher education; Higher education institutions
Accreditation Board for Engineering and Technology, 7–8
ACT Alumni Outcomes Survey, 11
ACT CAAP (Collegiate Assessment of Academic Proficiency) exam, 10
Action-centered leadership model: higher education curriculum application of, 48–51; illustrated diagram of, 47*fig*; overview of, 46–48
Adair, J., 45, 46, 47, 48, 49, 50
Adaptive Technology Lab (University of Washington), 35
AJAX, 95
Allen, I. E., 16
American Council on Education, 54, 60, 63
American Council of Educator's Fellows Program, 51
Americans with Disabilities Act (1990), 28, 40
Architectural Barriers Act (1968), 28
Assessment: Excellence in Higher Education (EHE) model for, 75–76; as higher education issue, 62–63
Associated Press, 35
Association of Commonwealth Universities, 54
Astin, A. W., 63

Baldrige, M., 65
Baldrige National Quality Award. *See* Malcolm Baldrige National Quality Award (MBNQA)
Bauer, R. A., 1, 5, 6, 13, 14, 98
Belohlav, J. A., 73

Bennett, W., 49
Bensimon, E., 49
Berdahl, R., 62
Birnbaum, R., 49
Boeke, M., 31
Bourke, A., 38
Bowe, F., 31
Boyer Commission, 60
Brancato, C. K., 64
Bremer, C. D., 40
Brown University, 36
Burgstahler, S., 35, 36, 41
Burke, J. C., 60, 63
Bush, G. W., 17
Business process execution language (BPEL), 95
Business process redesign (BPR), 90–91

Calhoun, J. M., 65
California Virtual University, 16
Canada's disability community, 40
CANARIE Inc. (Canada), 92
Capella University, 22
Caputo, A., 31, 32
Carey, K., 40
Carnevale, D., 16
CAST (Center for Applied Special Technology), 29–30, 33, 35, 40
Center for Creative Leadership, 54
Center on Postsecondary education and Disability (CPED) [University of Connecticut], 32, 39
Center for Universal Design, 28
Cermak, C., 59
Champy, J., 90
Chickering, A. W., 33
Collar, E., 6, 13
Collier, D. A., 67
Columbia University, 36
Columbus State Community College, 38
Commission on Higher Education report (2006), 36
Committee of Vice Chancellors and Principals (CVCP) [U.K.], 49, 51, 52
Communities of innovation: building higher education, 86; continuous communication of, 87; culture of trust in,

87–88; e-Strategy Framework (UBC) vision of, 88–89; removing barriers to effectiveness of, 86; services and collaboration of, 87. *See also* Innovation Community source software, 94–95
The Conference Room web site, 36
Connaughton, S. L., 73, 74
Cook, L. S., 73
Council for Excellence in Management and Leadership (U.K.), 52
Council for Higher Education Accreditation (CHEA), 63
Couturier, L. K., 60, 63
Cults of academic life, 51
Curphy, G., 47
Curriculum: action-centered leadership model used in leadership, 48–51; Western Governors University (WGU), 19–20. *See also* Universal design curriculum

Dalrymple, J. F., 8
Dartmouth College, 36
Demonstration Projects to Ensure Quality Higher Education for Students with Disabilities, 35
DETC (Distance Education and Training Council), 16, 18
Diamond, R. M., 101
Distance learning: national accreditation of, 16–17, 18–19; Western Governors University (WGU) format for, 16–24
DO-IT (University of Washington), 35–36, 41
Dodds, T., 2, 85, 95, 98
Dolan, R., 40
Donofrio, N. M., 100
Doumont, J., 35
Drucker, P., 1

e-Strategy Framework (UBC), 88–89
Eaton, J. S., 63, 64
Education for Handicapped Children Act (1975), 29
Education legislation, 28, 40
EHE Guide (Ruben), 71
Embry, P., 33
European Foundation for Quality Management, 65
European Quality Foundation Model, 65
European University Association, 54
Ewell, P., 60, 63
Excellence in Higher Education (EHE) model: application by leaders, 71; as assessment, planning, improvement guide, 71–73; illustrated diagram of, 70*fig;* knowledge and process outcomes using, 75*fig;* origins and elements of, 68–70; process of, 73*fig;* sample rating chart using, 72*fig;* value and impact of, 73–76
Excellence in Higher Education Guide (Ruben), 71

Facebook, 35
Facilitator's Guide (Rueben), 71
Faculty: training on teaching students with disabilities, 36–37; universal design training for, 37–38; Western Governors University (WGU) role of, 20–21
The Faculty Room Web site, 35
FacultyWare Web site (University of Connecticut), 40
Fair Housing Amendments Act (1988), 28
FAME (Faculty and Administrator Modules in Higher Education), 38
Farber, B., 28
Farber, S., 28
"Fast Facts for Faculty" project, 37
Fathom, 16
Fayol, H., 46
Field, K., 62
Fisher, W. W., 36
Flowers, Lord, 48–49
Flynn, B. B., 67
Foley, T. E., 39
Frank, R. H., 60, 63
Furmanski, P., 59
Furst-Bowe, J. A., 1, 5, 9, 13, 14, 68, 98

Gamson, Z. F., 33
Gardiner, L. F., 60
Garrett, R., 52
George Washington University, 38
Gibson, P., 40
Ginnett, R., 47
Glickman, T. S., 3, 97, 105
Goldsmith, M., 97
Government Accountability Office, 67
Graves, W. H., 35
Green, M., 45, 49
Grushina, Y., 59
Gruska, G. F., 67

Hammer, M., 90
Harvard University, 36
Heaphy, M. S., 67
Heiser, D. R., 73
Henderson, C., 31

Hesselbein, F., 97
High Education Funding Council for England, 51
Higher education: assessment issue of, 62–63; Excellence in Higher Education (EHE) model of, 68–70*fig*; innovation in context of, 97–98; innovation role in continuing development of, 98–99; societal gatekeeper role played by, 59–60; Spelling Commission on Future of, 35, 36, 40, 60–62, 98, 100. *See also* Accreditation
Higher Education Act, 17
Higher education institutions: belief systems or cults of academic life, 51; continuous review steps taken by, 102; facilitating innovation at, 5–6, 8–14; impact of education legislation on, 28, 40; keys to successful change management in, 12–13; leadership training by, 45–56. *See also* Accreditation
Higher Education Staff Development Agency (U.K.), 52
Higher Learning Commission (North Central Association of Colleges and Schools), 7
Hoisington, S. H., 6
Horn, L., 31
Horrigan, J., 35
Howell, D., 35
Hughes, R., 47
HungreyMinds, 16

Immordino K., 73, 74
Information technology: building communities of innovation through, 86–89; implementing infrastructure for, 91–94; improving business/academic processes using, 89–91; innovation facilitated through, 85–86, 99; trends in IT-driven innovation, 94–95
Innovation: cost pressures and impact on, 101–102; definition of, 5, 85, 98; efficiency and, 102–104; factors driving higher education, 5–6; flexibility of, 98–99; higher education context of, 97–98; information technology role in, 85–86, 99; keys to successful change management for, 12–13; lessons learned about facilitating, 13–14; in mature enterprise, 100–101; University of Wisconsin-Stout (UW-Stout) experience with, 8–12. *See also* Communities of innovation
Inside Higher Education, 60, 62

Institutional Leadership Project (U.K.), 49
Internet: communities of innovation through the, 86–89; as teaching tool, 35. *See also* Web sites
Iowa State University, 68
Ivy Access Initiative, 37, 39, 40
Izzo, M., 37

Jackson, N., 63
Jarratt Report (U.K.), 49
Java Architectures Special Interest Group (JA-SIG), 94
JM Associates, 90
Johnstone, C. J., 40, 41
Jurow, S., 5, 9, 59

Kaplan, R. S., 64
Kellogg Commission, 60
Kezar, A., 12
King, J.E., 31
Kinser, K., 2, 15, 16, 18, 22, 23, 25, 98
Korabik, K., 39
Kuh, G. D., 63

Lambert report (2003) [U.K.], 56
Lansing Community College, 38
Lawrence, F. L., 59, 60
Leadership development: action-centered (or functional) model of, 46–48; evolution of higher education, 45–46; Leadership Foundation work in area of, 2, 46, 52–56; moving forward agenda for, 48–52; themes used in work of, 48
Leadership Foundation for Higher Education (LFHE) [U.K.]: described, 52–53; developmental initiatives and opportunities of, 54; examples of activities undertaken by, 55*t*; innovative approach of, 2, 46, 99; organizational design and funding of, 53; role and positioning of, 54, 56; thematic and integrated focus of, 53–54
Leavitt, M., 17
Lederman, D., 62
Legislation (educational), 28, 40
Levine, A., 1
Lewin, K., 46
Light, R. J., 63
Lightfoot, E., 40
Lopez J., 73, 74
Lund, H., 63

McAlexander, P., 40
McDade, S., 45

Mace, R. L., 27, 28, 29
McGeveran, W., 36
McGregor, D., 47
McGuire, J. M., 32, 33, 34, 39, 40
McPherson, P., 62
Madaus, J. W., 39
Malcolm Baldrige National Quality Award Program (MBNQA): criteria for performance excellence, 6–7; Excellence in Higher Education (EHE) model based on, 68–70*fig*; flexibility and higher educational application of, 67–68; framework of, 65–67; higher education institutions awarded the, 8; impact on academic accreditation, 2, 7–8; linking accreditation and, 76–77; University of Wisconsin-Stout awarded the, 1, 8, 68, 98
Malcolm Baldrige National Quality Program, 5, 9, 65
Malveaux, J., 101
Marchese, T., 16
Maslow, A., 46
Massey, W. F., 8, 9, 11, 16, 60
Matheson, C., 45
Meyer, K. A., 16, 18, 23, 24
Middle States Commission on Higher Education, 63, 66
Middle States Commission of Schools and Colleges, 60, 63, 68
Middlehurst, R., 2, 45, 48, 49, 51, 52, 57
Miller, C., 62
Minassians, H., 63
Moen, D., 5, 9, 13, 14
Monfort College of Business (University of Northern Colorado), 8
Morrill Act (1862), 98
Mueller, J. L., 28, 29
Munitz, B., 60
Murray, A., 37
MySpace, 35

National Association of State Universities and Land-Grant Colleges, 60
National Center for Public Policy and Education, 100
National Council for Accreditation of Teacher Education, 7–8
National Institute for Standards and Technology (NIST), 65, 67
National Report Card on Higher Education (2006), 100
Nelson, B., 17
Neumann, A., 49

Nevill, S., 31
Newman, F., 60, 63
No Child Left Behind Act, 22
North Central Association of Colleges and Schools, 7, 63, 66, 68
Northwest Association of Schools and Colleges, 16
Northwest Commission on Colleges and Universities, 63
Norton, D. P., 64

Observatory on Borderless Higher Education (OBHE), 54
Office of Post Secondary Education, 35
Ohio Learning Network, 38
Ohio State University (OSU), 37
Ohio State University Partnership Grant, 37
Organization for Economic Cooperation and Development, 53
OXO Good Grips, 28
OXO International, 28

Palmer, J., 32, 39
Pascarella, E. T., 63
Paulson, K., 31
Piper, M., 88
Plato's Academy (ancient Greece), 98
Pope, M., 49, 51
Procter, E., 39
Przasnyski, Z., 65, 67
Pursuing Excellence in Higher Education: Eight Fundamental Challenges (Ruben), 62

Rajan, M., 67
Ramsden, P., 50
Rehabilitation Act (1973), 28
Rhodes, C., 59
Richland College (Texas), 8, 68
Rio Salado College (Arizona), 101
Romboy, D., 18
Ruben, B. D., 2, 7, 59, 60, 63, 64, 65, 67, 69, 71, 72, 73, 83
Russ, T., 73, 74
Rutgers University, 68, 73

Saladin, B., 67
Sandmeyer, L., 59
Scarpino, A., 38
Schray, V., 62, 63, 65
Scott, S. S., 32, 33, 34, 39, 40
Seaman, J., 16
Section 504 (Rehabilitation Act), 28
Selingo, J., 63
Serban, A. M., 60, 63

Service-oriented architecture (SOA), 94
"Seven Principles for Good Practice in Undergraduate Education" (Chickering and Gamson), 33
Seymour, D. T., 63
Shaw, R., 37, 39
Shaw, S. F., 32, 39
Silver, P., 38
Simons, T., 35
Smulowitz, S. M., 73, 74
Snider, M., 35
Somerville, I., 97
Sorensen, C. W., 5, 9, 12, 13, 14
Southern Association of Colleges and Schools, 63, 64, 66, 68, 76
Southern Association of Colleges and Schools Commission on Colleges, 7
Spangehl, S. D., 7, 63
Spelling Commission on the Future of Higher Education, 35, 36, 40, 60–62, 98, 100
Spellings, M., 60, 62, 63, 65
Srikanthan, G., 8
Standing Conference of Principals (U.K.), 46
Stanford University, 36
Stogdill, R., 47
Story, M. F., 28, 29
Strehorn, K. C., 38
Student Monitor survey (2006), 35
Students: survey on preferences of, 35; universal design curriculum response to diversity of, 31–34, 40–41
Students with disabilities: education legislation on, 28, 40; training faculty to effectively teach, 36–37; universal design curriculum meeting needs of, 35–36
SWOT analysis, 9

Tagg, J., 6, 12
Tai, L. S., 65, 67
Tamimi, N., 67
Tang, V., 6, 13
Teaching Every Student in the Digital Age: Universal Design for Learning (CAST), 40
Teaching Support Services (TSS) [University of Guelph], 31–32, 39
Technology: consortia benefits from, 103–104; distance learning application of, 16; higher education innovation through information, 85–95; universal design curriculum role of, 34–36, 99

Terenzini, P. T., 63
Thompson, S. J., 40, 41
Thurlow, M. L., 40, 41
"To Reclaim a Legacy" (Bennett), 49
Top Management Programme for Higher Education (U.K.), 51
Torres, K., 38
Tufte, E., 35
Twigg, C. A., 35

UID interactive quiz, 40
U.K. Department of Education and Science (DES), 48
U.K. Department of Trade and Industry, 97
UNESCO, 53
Universal design curriculum: CAST application of, 29–30, 33, 35; challenges and implications of, 38–40; Chickering and Gamson's nine principles for, 33–34; expanding role of technology in, 34–36, 99; fiscal promise of, 102; impact of education legislation on, 28, 40; Mace's seven principles governing concept of, 28–29; origins and development of, 27–28; political and assessment pressures on, 36–38; student diversity impact on, 31–34; Teaching Support Services (TSS) application of, 31–32; various acronyms used for, 29. See also Curriculum
Universal Design in Education: Teaching Nontraditional Students (Bowe), 31
Universal design for instruction (UDI), 29, 32–33
Universal design for learning (UDL), 29, 30
Universal instructional design (UID), 29
Universities UK, 46, 52, 54
University of British Columbia (UBC): building community of innovation at, 86–88; e-Strategy Framework of, 88–89; network infrastructure at, 92–93
University of Connecticut, 32, 39, 40
University of Guelph (Canada), 31, 32, 39, 40
University of London, 48
University of Missouri-Rolla, 68
University of Northern British Columbia, 93
University of Northern Colorado, 8
University of Northern Colorado's Monfort School of Business, 68
University of Phoenix, 22

University of Surrey (U.K.), 45, 47
University of Washington, 41
University of Washington's Adaptive
 Technology Lab, 35
University of Wisconsin-Stout (UW-Stout):
 Baldrige National Quality Award to, 1,
 8, 68, 98; innovation at the, 8–12
U.S. Department of Education, 62, 98,
 100, 101
U.S. Department of Education Distance
 Education Demonstration Program, 17
U.S. Department of Education and Nati-
 onal Center for Education Statistics, 31
UW-Stout Chancellor's Advisory Council,
 9, 10
UW-Stout Curriculum Innovation Center,
 10
UW-Stout Strategic Planning Group, 10

Vaneswaran, S. A., 6
Vokurka, R. J., 65

Walden University, 22
Ward, D., 62
Web sites: CAST, 40; The Conference
 Room, 36; The Faculty Room, 35;
 FacultyWare (University of Connecti-
 cut), 40; FAME, 38; Ivy Access Initia-
 tive, 40; Teaching Every Student in the
 Digital Age: (CAST), 40; UID quiz, 40.
 See also Internet

Weinstein, L. A., 60
Wentz, M., 68
West Chester University, 38
Western Association of Schools and
 Colleges, 63, 64
Western Governors University (WGU):
 changing identity of, 17–19; curricu-
 lum of, 19–20; fiscal promise of, 101;
 innovative approach of, 1–2, 99; mar-
 ket and mission of, 21–23; national
 accreditation of, 16–17, 18–19; new
 faculty role at, 20–21; origins and devel-
 opment of, 15–17; success of, 23–24,
 103
WGU Teacher Education program, 17
White, S. C., 3, 97, 105
Wikipedia, 85
Wilson, D. D., 67
Wilson, R., 60, 63
Wingspread Group on Higher Education,
 60
Workbook and Scoring Manual (Ruben),
 71
World Bank, 46, 53
Wray, M., 49, 51

Yuval, L., 39

Zeff, R., 2, 27, 44, 98
Zemsky, R., 16

NEW DIRECTIONS FOR HIGHER EDUCATION
Order Form
SUBSCRIPTIONS AND SINGLE ISSUES

DISCOUNTED BACK ISSUES:

*Use this form to receive **20% off** all back issues of New Directions for Higher Education. All single issues priced at **$23.20** (normally $29.00)*

TITLE   ISSUE NO.   ISBN

_____   _____   _____

_____   _____   _____

_____   _____   _____

***Call 888-378-2537** or see mailing instructions below. When calling, mention the promotional code, JB7ND, to receive your discount.*

SUBSCRIPTIONS: *(1 year, 4 issues)*

☐ New Order   ☐ Renewal

U.S.	☐ Individual: $80	☐ Institutional: $195
Canada/Mexico	☐ Individual: $80	☐ Institutional: $235
All Others	☐ Individual: $104	☐ Institutional: $269

***Call 888-378-2537** or see mailing and pricing instructions below. Online subscriptions are available at www.interscience.wiley.com.*

Copy or detach page and send to:
John Wiley & Sons, Journals Dept, 5th Floor
989 Market Street, San Francisco, CA 94103-1741

Order Form can also be faxed to: 888-481-2665

	SHIPPING CHARGES:		
Issue/Subscription Amount: $ _____			
Shipping Amount: $ _____	SURFACE	Dometic	Canadian
(for single issues only—subscription prices include shipping)	First Item	$5.00	$6.00
Total Amount: $ _____	Each Add'l Item	$3.00	$1.50

(No sales tax for U.S. subscriptions. Canadian residents, add GST for subscription orders. Individual rate subscriptions must be paid by personal check or credit card. Individual rate subscriptions may not be resold as library copies.)

☐ Payment enclosed (U.S. check or money order only. All payments must be in U.S. dollars.)

☐ VISA   ☐ MC   ☐ Amex # _____ Exp. Date _____

Card Holder Name _____ Card Issue # _____

Signature_____ Day Phone _____

☐ Bill Me (U.S. institutional orders only. Purchase order required.)

Purchase order # _____
                Federal Tax ID13559302   GST 89102 8052

Name_____

Address _____

Phone _____ E-mail _____

JB7ND

Your guide to serving a new generation of students.

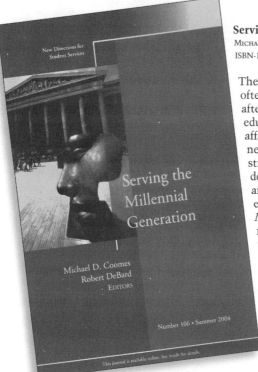

Serving the Millenial Generation
MICHAEL D. COOMES AND ROBERT DEBARD, EDITORS
ISBN-10: 0-7879-7606-7 • $28.00

The Millennial Generation, often categorized as those born after 1981, will require higher education leaders and student affairs practitioners to adopt new learning and service strategies, rethink student development theories, and modify educational environments. *Serving the Millennial Generation* gives readers the foundation for understanding this newest generation of students and to offer suggestions on how to educate and serve them more effectively.

Table of Contents:

1. A Generational Approach to Understanding Students
MICHAEL D. COOMES AND ROBERT DEBARD

2. Understanding the Historical and Cultural Influences That Shape Generations
MICHAEL D. COOMES

3. Millennials Coming to College ROBERT DEBARD

4. Constructions of Student Development Across the Generations
C. CARNEY STRANGE

5. Teaching, Learning, and Millennial Students
MAUREEN E. WILSON

6. Understanding Diversity in Millennial Students
ELLEN M. BROIDO

7. Student Affairs for a New Generation
JOHN WESLEY LOWERY

Serving the Millennial Generation is a best-selling issue of the quarterly report *New Directions for Student Services*. Subscriptions can be ordered by calling 888-378-2537.

**NEW DIRECTIONS FOR HIGHER EDUCATION
IS NOW AVAILABLE ONLINE AT WILEY INTERSCIENCE**

What is Wiley InterScience?

Wiley InterScience is the dynamic online content service from John Wiley &
Sons delivering the full text of over 300 leading scientific, technical, medical,
and professional journals, plus major reference works, the acclaimed *Current
Protocols* laboratory manuals, and even the full text of select Wiley print books
online.

What are some special features of Wiley InterScience?

Wiley InterScience Alerts is a service that delivers table of contents via e-mail
for any journal available on Wiley InterScience as soon as a new issue is
published online.
Early View is Wiley's exclusive service presenting individual articles online as
soon as they are ready, even before the release of the compiled print issue.
These articles are complete, peer-reviewed, and citable.
CrossRef is the innovative multi-publisher reference linking system enabling
readers to move seamlessly from a reference in a journal article to the cited
publication, typically located on a different server and published by a different
publisher.

How can I access Wiley InterScience?

Visit http://www.interscience.wiley.com

Guest Users can browse Wiley InterScience for unrestricted access to journal
Tables of Contents and Article Abstracts, or use the powerful search engine.
Registered Users are provided with a *Personal Home Page* to store and
manage customized alerts, searches, and links to favorite journals and articles.
Additionally, Registered Users can view free Online Sample Issues and preview
selected material from major reference works.
Licensed Customers are entitled to access full-text journal articles in PDF, with
select journals also offering full-text HTML.

How do I become an Authorized User?

Authorized Users are individuals authorized by a paying Customer to have
access to the journals in Wiley InterScience. For example, a university that
subscribes to Wiley journals is considered to be the Customer. Faculty, staff and
students authorized by the university to have access to those journals in Wiley
InterScience are Authorized Users. Users should contact their Library for information on which Wiley journals they have access to in Wiley InterScience.

ASK YOUR INSTITUTION ABOUT WILEY INTERSCIENCE TODAY!